7037

The Scud

and other Russian Ballistic Missile Vehicles

Text & Scale Drawings by Steven Zaloga
Color plates by Arkadiusz Wróbel

603-609 Castle Peak Road
Kong Nam Industrial Building
10/F, B1, Tsuen Wan
New Territories, Hong Kong
www.concord-publications.com

We welcome authors who can help expand our range of books. If you would like to submit material, please feel free to contact us.

We are always on the look-out for new, unpublished photos for this series.
If you have photos or slides or information you feel may be useful to future volumes, please send them to us for possible future publication.
Full photo credits will be given upon publication.

ISBN 962-361-675-9
printed in Hong Kong

Introduction

Mobile ballistic missile vehicles are among the world's most powerful weapons. They combine the nuclear power of missiles with the mobility and survivability of tracked or wheeled launch vehicles. This type of mobile weapon system was especially popular in the former Soviet Union, and remains an essential element of the Russian armed forces today. This book takes a look at the wide range of Soviet and Russian ballistic missile vehicles, from the small divisional rocket artillery systems such as the FROG-7, to mobile intercontinental missiles such as the SS-25 Sickle. This book contains some of the first published photographs of many of the secret and lesser known vehicles. Soviet mobile ballistic missiles have been mentioned frequently in the news over the past decade both in regards to arms control talks and in accounts of regional conflicts. Until recently, the Soviet Union was the only country which extensively exported ballistic missiles. As a result, nearly all ballistic missiles fired in combat since the end of World War 2 have been Soviet missiles or those based on Soviet designs. The Scud is the most famous of these because of its use in the 1991 Gulf War, but other types, such as the FROG-7, have also seen extensive combat employment.

Missile Designations

There is considerable confusion over the names and designations of Soviet missiles and their associated equipment. Until recently, the Russian names and designations for most of their missile systems were not known. So the best known designations in the West are those applied by US and NATO intelligence agencies. The US Director of Central Intelligence's Weapons and Space Systems Intelligence Committee (WSSIC) applies a numerical designation when a Soviet missile is first spotted. For ballistic missiles, this begins with an SS- suffix, such as SS-21, meaning surface-to-surface; or FROG (Free Rocket Over Ground) for unguided rockets. The NATO Air Standardization Coordinating Committee (ASCC) separately applies a codename to the weapon system, beginning in "S" for ballistic missiles, such as Scarab. The ASCC system is related to the aircraft naming system (Fishbed for MiG-21, etc.) These two are often used together such as SS-21 Scarab.

The Russians have a variety of designations for missile systems. Often, the weapon system has a project name during development, such as Tochka (Point) for the SS-21 Scarab. When the missile is accepted for army use by a state commission, it is often given a designation such as R-17 for the SS-1c Scud B missile. These designations are usually classified, so when the project transitions to industrial production, an unclassified industrial index number is given to the weapon by the GURVO (Main Directorate for Missile Weapons). In the case of artillery rockets and missiles, this begins with the prefix 9M for the missile itself, 9K for the overall system, 9P for the launcher, and 9T for the transloader. Other numbering systems apply as well, for example, the 15Zhxx designations for strategic solid fuel ballistic missiles, 3Mxx for naval missiles, etc. To confuse matters, some of the older systems use an earlier pattern of industrial index numbers, such as the 3R designations for early FROG rockets and the 8K designation for early ballistic missile systems. In this book, every attempt has been made to identify the equipment by its proper Soviet designations, as well as by the appropriate US WSSIC codes and NATO ASCC codenames. The list below is intended to provide a quick guide to the systems covered in this book.

US WSSIC	*NATO ASCC*	*Russian Name*	*Russian Bureau Number*	*GURVO System Index*	*GURVO Missile Index*	*GURVO Launcher Index*
SS-1 a	Scunner	Yedinichka	R-1A	8A11		
SS-1 b	Scud A	-	R-11, R-150	8K11		8U218
SS-1c	Scud B	-	R-17	8K14		2P19
SS-1c	Scud B	Zemlya	R-17, R-300	9K72	9M72	2P20, 9P117
SS-12	Scaleboard	Temp	TR-1	9K71	9M71	2P11
SS-12 (SS-22)	Scaleboard	Temp-S		9K76	9M76	9P120
SS-14	Scamp/ Scapegoat	-	RT-15	8K96		ob. 815
SS-15	Scrooge	-	RT-20	8K99		ob. 821
SS-20	Saber	Pioner			15Zh45	15P72
SS-21	Scarab	Tochka		9K79	9M79	9P129
SS-23	Spider	Oka	R-400	9K714	9M714	9P71
SS-25	Sickle	Topol	RT-2PM		15Zh58	
SS-26	Stone	Tender				
SS-27		Topol-M	RT-2PM2			
FROG-1	-	Filin	3R-2	-		2P4
FROG-2	-	Mars	3R-1	-		2P2
FROG-3	-	Luna	3R-8	2K6		2P16
FROG-5	-	Luna-2	3R-10	2K6		2P16
FROG-7a	-	Luna-M	3R-11/R-65	9K52	9M21	9P113
FROG-7b	-	Luna-M	R-70	9K52	9M21	9P113
SSC-1a	Sepal	Progress	FKR-2		9M12	2P30
SSC-1 b	Shaddock	Redut	S-35	4K95	3M44	SPU-35V
SSC-3	Styx	Rubezh-A	P-20, P-21	4K51	3M51	3P51
SSC-4	Slingshot	Granat	S-10		3M12	

Russian Mobile Missiles

The Soviet armed forces, and today's Russian Army have two branches armed with mobile ballistic missile systems. The Ground Forces employ tactical ballistic missiles such as the FROG-7 and the SS-21 Scarab in their armored and mechanized division. Longer-ranged tactical missiles, such as the SS-1c Scud, the SS-12 Scaleboard and the SS-23 Spider, were employed at army and front level but most of these have been retired. The Strategic Missile Forces (RVSN) have deployed strategic weapons for regional targeting such as the SS-20 Saber and for intercontinental objectives, such as the SS-24 Scalpel and the SS-25 Sickle.

The first Soviet ballistic missile units formed in 1947 were equipped with mobile missiles. The early units, such as the 23rd Guards Special Operations Brigade, were equipped with captured German equipment, the famous V-2 ballistic missile, mounted on FMS railroad launchers. These units were later equipped with mobile ballistic missiles of Soviet manufacture, derived from German missile technology such as the R-1 (SS-1a Scunner) and R-2 (SS-2 Sibling). As was the case with the German V-2, these were fired from mobile trailers, based on the German Meillerwagen. In the 1950s, the Soviet Main Artillery Administration (GAU) began developing self-propelled ballistic missile launchers, primarily intended for the delivery of tactical nuclear weapons. In later years, these missiles were adapted to carry conventional and chemical warheads, but nuclear weapons delivery has been one of the primary requirements of this class of weapons.

Divisional Artillery Rockets

Development of unguided artillery rockets capable of delivering nuclear weapons began in the mid-1950s. The first of these was completed in 1955 and was designated FROG-1 (Free-Rocket-Over-Ground-1) by NATO. It's Soviet designation was 3R-2 Filin (Eagle owl). This rocket was launched from a special tracked transporter-erector-launcher (TEL) based on the ISU-152 heavy assault gun chassis called the Obiekt 804 and later, 2P4 Tyulpan (Tulip). Very few of these vehicles were manufactured, and this missile system was quickly replaced by more modern designs. The Filin was developed alongside a lighter artillery rocket system called the 3R-1 Mars. This rocket was launched from a chassis derived from the PT-76 amphibious tank called the 2P2. Like the Filin, the Mars was built in very small numbers, with only 25 produced. The Mars was issued in modest numbers to composite rocket artillery battalions in key tank divisions. These battalions had two Mars launchers and two BMD-20 multiple rocket launchers.

These early artillery rockets were followed by the Luna (moon) series of rockets. The first of these, the FROG-3, appeared in 1957. It was designated *Luna-1* (Moon-1) in the Soviet Ground Forces. This series used the improved 2P16 TEL, which could be distinguished from the earlier 2P2 TEL by its use of a modified suspension with return rollers. The Luna family included three different rockets, the original 3R-9 (FROG-3) with a 3N15 conventional high explosive warhead, and the 3R-10 (FROG-5) which could carry a 400 kg 3N14 nuclear warhead. The FROG-4 designation applied to a variant of the FROG-5 with a barometric nose probe which does not appear to have been commonly deployed. All these rockets were fired from the same launcher system. Of the three types, the 3R-9 and 3R-10 were the only types exported to other members of the Warsaw Pact. In total, about 200 Luna-1 and Luna-2 rocket vehicles were in Soviet service by the early 1960s. The FROG-6 designation was given to a truck-mounted training rocket.

The Luna series was followed by the far more successful 9K52 *Luna-M* series, known in the West as FROG-7. The Luna-M is based on the ZiL-135LTM six-wheeled truck, rather than on a tracked chassis. The basic launcher vehicle is designated the 9P113. There is a specialized transloader vehicles, also based on the ZiL-135, designated the 9T29. The Luna-M first began entering service in 1965 and is the most numerous Soviet mobile missile system with over 750 in service when peak strength was reached in 1986. The original version of the Luna-M used the 3R-11 rocket, later redesignated R-65 and finally as 9M21. This type was called FROG-7a by NATO. In 1968, an improved rocket was developed, called R-70 (FROG-7b). This version has a lengthened fuselage and was the standard version of this weapon system. The FROG-7 does not have a guidance system, relying instead on spin-stabilization. So it is classified as an artillery rocket rather than as a guided missile. The FROG-7 has been widely exported and has been used by about 15 countries, including the former Warsaw Pact armies. It has been widely used in combat since its combat debut in the 1973 Mid-East War. It was used in large numbers in Afghanistan, in the 1980-88 Iran-Iraq war, in the 1991 Gulf War, and in many other conflicts.

In 1975, a replacement for the FROG-7 began to appear in Soviet service, the 9K79 Tochka (Point), better known by its US/NATO code-name, SS-21 Scarab. The Tochka is a far more sophisticated missile than the Luna-M, closely resembling the American MGM-140 ATACMS. It uses a sophisticated inertial guidance system, giving it far greater accuracy than the FROG-7. Its BAZ-5921 TEL is a relative of the BAZ-5937 chassis used with the SA-8 Gecko (Osa-M) air defense missile vehicle. It is built by the Lenin TMS Plant in Petropavlovsk. The 9T218 transloader vehicle which carries two reload missiles and a reload crane, is based on a nearly identical vehicle, the BAZ-5922. Although the 9M79 missile can be fitted with both nuclear and chemical warheads, the Tochka is the first Soviet divisional artillery missile to have the accuracy to employ a conventional warhead effectively. Indeed, the Tochka is sometimes called the "Patriot buster" since one of its wartime requirements was the ability to attack the deadly Patriot air defense missile in advance of aircraft attacks. The threat posed by the Tochka led to the Patriot PAC-1 and PAC-2 anti-missile variants which were used against the Scud during Operation Desert Storm. Due to the disruption of Soviet missile artillery forces by the INF Treaty, and retirement of many older missiles such as the Scud, there has been a reorganization of Russian tactical ballistic missile systems. Although originally intended as a divisional system, many Tochka missile systems have been "booted upstairs" into new army or front level missile brigades. The Tochka has been exported to Syria and several other countries. It was first used in combat during the fighting in Chechnya in November 1999, where more than 130 missiles were launched into the city of Grozniy over a few weeks time.

Divisional Artillery Rockets and Missiles Technical Data

Russian name	Filin	Mars	Luna	Luna-M	Tochka
Western name	FROG-1	FROG-2	FROG-3/5	FROG-7	SS-21 Scarab
IOC	1955	1955	1961	1965	1971
TEL Chassis	IS-2	PT-76	PT-76 mod	ZiL-135/BAZ-135	BAZ-5921
TEL designation	2P4 Tyulpan	2P2	2P16	9P113	9P129

TEL weight (T)	36.5	14.2	14.2	23.0	18.1
TEL length (m)	10.7	9.4	10.5	10.7	9.48
TEL width (m)	3.2	3.18	3.18	2.8	2.78
TEL height (m)	3.32	3.05	3.05	3.66	2.37
Engine	V-2IS	V-6	V-6	ZIL-135	5D20B
Horsepower	520	240	240	360	200
Road speed (km/h)	37	44	44	65	60
Reaction time (min)	30	15-30	15-3030	15-30	15
Refire time (min)	60	60	60	60	65-70
Transloader	-	2P3	2U663	9T29	9T218

Rocket/Missile Data

Designation	3R-2	3R-1	3R-10	3R-11 /9M21	9M79
Weight (T)	3.17	2.45	2.28	2.3	2.0
Length (m)	10.2	9.4	10.6	8.95/9.4	6.4
Diameter (m)	.84	.58	.54	.55	.65
Warhead (kg)	1180	545	503	420-457	482
Max.range (km)	32	19	32	65	70
Min.range (km)	20	15	10	15	15
CEP (m)	1000	900	880	500-700	50-100
Guidance	spin	spin	spin	spin	inertial

Army & Front Ballistic Missiles

The first Soviet tactical missile developed to deliver a tactical nuclear warhead was the R-11, better known in the West as the SS-1b Scud A. This missile was intended to replace the earlier R-1A and R-2 missiles which were derived from the German V-2. The R-11 had a completely different propulsion system using hypergolic rather than cryogenic fuel, based on the German Wasserfall missile engine. It was designed to be simpler, more economical and more reliable than the older missiles.

The R-11 missile was launched from a TEL based on the ISU-152 assault gun called the 8U218. The complete weapon system was designated 8K11 by the Soviet army. It entered service in the mid-1950s, equipping army-level missile brigades. Its main use was to deliver tactical nuclear warheads against targets deeper in the rear than could be reached by the Luna rockets or by artillery.

In 1955, an improved missile, the R-17 entered development. It was first test flown in the spring of 1957. The R-17 missile used a modified version of the 8U218, now designated 2P19 when using the R-17 missile. This was called the SS-1c Scud B by NATO when it entered service in 1961 but it was not built in large numbers. The tracked 2P19 was obsolete by the late 1950s as heavy tank production ended. As a result, it was decided to move to a more reliable TEL based on the MAZ-543 eight-wheel heavy transporter. This new TEL was designated 2P20, and later 9P113 Uragan (Hurricane), but it is more popularly called *Kashalot* (Sperm Whale) by its Russian crews. The 8K14 system was later redesignated 9K72 Elbrus in the 1980s, and the R-17 missile became designated the R-300.

The 8K11 variant was exported to several of the Warsaw Pact countries, but was not widely exported outside of Europe. The Scuds exported to the Mid-East were provided with the newer 9P113 TEL. The Scud B was first used in combat in the 1973 Mid-East war when Egyptian Scud battalions fired at Israeli targets in the Sinai desert. The Scud first became famous for its role in the 1986-88 "war of the cities" during the fighting between Iran and Iraq. The Scud became even more infamous during the 1991 Gulf War when longer-ranged Iraqi Al-Husayn (600 km) and Al-Hijarah (750 km) variants were fired against targets in Saudi Arabia and Israel. These missiles used lightened warheads and extended fuselages with larger fuel tanks to increase their range. The most extensive use of the Scud was in the later years of the Afghanistan war, where over 1,000 of these missiles were fired against villages loyal to the mujihadeen resistance.

The Scud was supposed to be replaced in the 1980s by the new Oka (SS-23 Spider). The Oka was developed by the KBM design bureau in Kolomna which also developed the Tochka. So the systems have many similarities and the 9P71 wheeled TEL resembles an enlarged Tochka 9P129. The Oka had very little impact on the Soviet missile forces, as it soon fell under the range requirements of the Intermediate Nuclear Forces (INF) Treaty between the US and USSR. As a result, the Oka was in Soviet army service for only a few years before the missiles were withdrawn and destroyed under the terms of the INF Treaty. The Oka was also exported to East Germany, Czechoslovakia and Bulgaria. The Germans, Czechs and Slovaks agreed to destroy their missiles unilaterally, but the Bulgarians refused. The small number of Bulgarian Oka are the only surviving examples of this highly sophisticated ballistic missile system, except for several demilitarized museum displays. An improved version of the Oka has been developed in recent years, called the Iskander in its export version and the Tender in its Russian army version. The original version was fired from a vehicle very similar to the Oka, but the production version carries two missile launch rails and is mounted on a larger truck chassis.

The longest range ballistic missile in service with the Soviet Ground Forces was the Temp, better known in the West as the SS-12 Scaleboard. This system is based on the 2P11 TEL using the MAZ-543 truck, so it is easy to mistake for the Scud. The original versions of the system fired the 9M71 missile, known as SS-12a Scaleboard by NATO. In the 1980s, the improved 9M79 missile and 9P120 TEL entered service, first known as SS-22 by NATO but later reclassified as SS-12b. These weapons also fell under the range limitations of the INF Treaty, and so were destroyed in 1989-1990. There have been many reports of these missiles being exported. But in fact, this was never the case.

Army and Front Ballistic Missile Technical Data

US Designation	SS-1b	SS-1c	SS-12/SS-22	SS-23
NATO Codename	Scud A	Scud B	Scaleboard	Spider
System Designation	8K11	9K72	9K71/9K79	9K714
System Name		Elbrus	Temp/Temp-S	Oka
IOC	1956	1962	1965/1979	1986
TEL Data				
TEL Chassis	ISU-152	MAZ-543	MAZ-543	BAZ-6944
Weight (T)	38	29.0	30.8	24.07
Length (m)	12.5	13.58	13.15	11.76
Width (m)	3.2	3.02	3.02	3.13
Height (m)	3.32	3.7	3.5	3.00
Engine	V-2IS	D-12A	D-12A	D-144
Horsepower	520	525	525	580
Road speed (km/h)	37	70	70	70
Missile Data				
Missile designation	R-11	R-17/R-300	TR-1	R-400
Missile index number		9M72	9M71/9M79	9M714
Weight (T)	4.5	6.37	9.8	4.99
Length (m)	10.7	11.2	12.78	7.52
Diameter (m)	.84	.84	1.01	.97
Warhead weight (kg)	680	770	1000	1000
Range (km)	150	280	900	400
Fuel	Liquid	Liquid	Solid	Solid

Mobile Strategic Missiles

The Soviet RVSN strategic missile force considered the option of placing some of its missiles on mobile launchers to enhance their survivability instead of other defensive means such as silos. The first of these programs involved intermediate range ballistic missiles (IRBM), targeted on western Europe and China and Japan. The first example of one of these systems was the SS-14 Scamp, developed first by the Korolev design bureau, and completed by the new MIT Design Bureau in the early 1960s. It was mounted on a heavy tracked chassis using components from the T-10 heavy tank. The missile was a derivative of the RS-12 (SS-13 Savage).

The first successful Soviet mobile IRBM was the Pioner, better known by its US/NATO code-name, SS-20 Saber. The Pioner is a solid-fuel missile launched from a canister mounted on a MAZ-547V heavy transporter. The TEL vehicle was developed by the Titan TsKB at the Barrikady Plant in Volgograd. The TEL normally operates from a special Krona hanger with an opening roof. The missile can be launched from within the hanger, or the vehicle can transport the missile to a more distant location for firing. The Pioner/SS-20 fell under the range limits of the INF Treaty, and so they were dismantled or destroyed with the exception of a small number of museum exhibits and missiles retained for space launches.

In the early 1960's, the first of the mobile intercontinental ballistic missiles (ICBM) was first tested, the SS-15 Scrooge. This system was not successful, and was never operationally deployed. In the mid-1960s, it was followed by the 15Zh42 Temp-2S (SS-16 Sinner). The Temp-2S used a heavy wheeled transporter, based on the MAZ-547 series. This vehicle has never been shown, so details are lacking. A total of seven regiments were deployed with about 40 launchers. It served as the basis for a reduced range intermediate range missile, the Pioner (SS-20) which was mentioned above. The first successful Soviet mobile intercontinental missile was the Topol (Poplar Tree; SS-25 Sickle). It was developed from the Pioner, having an additional stage added to give it the added range. The TEL vehicle has had an extra axle added, but otherwise resembles the earlier Pioner TEL. The Topol is currently one of the most modern missiles in the Russian strategic arsenal, and is being followed by an improved derivative called the Topol-M (SS-27).

Other Mobile Surface-to-Surface Missile Systems

Although not mobile ballistic missiles, strictly speaking, this book also contains coverage of surface-to-surface cruise missile launcher vehicles. It seems appropriate to include these in this book since they are based on the same chassis as common ballistic missile TELs and fulfill a related role.

The FKR-2 (SSC-1a Sepal) is usually mistaken as the similar Navy Redut (SSC-1b Shaddock) coastal anti-ship missile system. However, it was in fact deployed by the Soviet air force in the tactical nuclear delivery role until it was retired in the late 1960s as more satisfactory strike aircraft such as the Su-24 Fencer became available.

The earliest Soviet coastal anti-ship launchers, such as the S-2 Sopka (SS-C-2b Samlet) were fired from towed trailers. These were soon supplemented by more mobile launchers, based on the ZiL-135 truck, firing the S-35 (SSC-1b Sepal) cruise missile. The Soviet Ground Forces use a modified version of this launcher for their Reys reconnaissance drone.

These two types of launchers were the most common coastal missile launchers through the 1970s. In the late 1970s, the Rubezh system was first deployed. The Rubezh system combined the tried-and-tested P-20/P-21 (SS-N-2 Styx) anti-ship missile, with a compact mobile launcher. The new launcher system, dubbed SSC-3 by NATO, carries two Styx missiles on a modified MAZ-543M chassis. For longer ranged targets, the 3K10 Granat system was developed. This launcher, also based on a modified MAZ-543 chassis, carries four cruise missiles. These cruise missiles are the equivalent of the US Navy's Tomahawk system. The Granat system was eliminated under the terms of the INF Treaty hardly having entered service.

The first Soviet tactical rocket system was the Filin (FROG-1), developed around 1955. It used the simple 3R-2 unguided artillery rocket, designed to be large enough to incorporate a nuclear warhead. The 2P4 Tyulpan (Tulip) launcher vehicle was based on the ISU-152 heavy assault gun chassis, called the Obiekt 804.

A rear view of the 2P4 Tyulpan launchers during one of the periodic parades in Red Square in Moscow. As is evident from the rear view, the 3R-2 rocket was powered by seven small solid fuel rocket engines, one of the reasons for its inefficiency.

An overhead view of the Filin's 2P4 Tyulpan launcher vehicle. The heavy weight and unimpressive performance of the 3R-2 rocket led to its quick demise. It was never used in large numbers by the Soviet Ground Forces.

The first modern tactical rocket system in Soviet Ground Forces use was the Mars, known in the West as the FROG-2. It can be distinguished from the later models by the shape of the 3R-1 rocket warhead. The nuclear warhead needed to be kept at a set temperature, so was surrounded by a heated liquid resulting in the large swelled cover. The 2P2 TEL differs from later Luna versions in the suspension, which is a modified PT-76 light tank chassis.

The Mars rocket system was not widely deployed, only about 25 being built. This is a rare view of one of the 2P2 launcher vehicles in use in the 1960s. The associated reload vehicle was called the 2P3 and 25 of those were built to service the launcher vehicles.

The first tactical rocket systems to enter service in any quantity was the 2K6 Luna series. The US/NATO codename of FROG-3, FROG-4 and FROG-5 implies that there were three systems. In fact, there was only one system, but three slightly different rockets. The 3R-9 rocket seen here was known as the FROG-5 and was armed with the 3N15 high explosive warhead. The cabling on the side of the vehicle leads to a remote launch control panel. The launcher vehicle, the 2P16, was based on the PT-76 light tank chassis, but had a modified suspension with return rollers.

A Polish Luna with 3R-9 rocket being prepared for firing. The artillery survey post resting against the front of the vehicle is a reminder that the 3R2 rocket was unguided: it required precise positioning like an artillery piece in order to have even a minimum degree of accuracy. These rockets had CEP (Circular Error Probabilities) of 800 meters, meaning that only 50% of the rockets would strike within a circle measuring 800 meters (1/2 mile) around their intended target. This poor accuracy was acceptable when a nuclear warhead was used, but they were not practical bombardment weapons when using conventional warheads.

A parade of Polish 2P16 Luna TEL with the 3R-9 (FROG-5) rocket in Warsaw. The launchers are marked with the white Piast eagle national insignia, dating this photo to the 1960s. The Warsaw Pact forces had rocket systems with nuclear capability, but the warheads were kept under Soviet custody.

The 2P16 Luna with 3R-9 rocket is one of the more widely preserved types in eastern European museums. This is a 2P16 kept at the Central Army Museum in Moscow with a World War II armored train behind it. The 2P16 launcher vehicle introduced a number of improvements over the older 2P2 Mars chassis. This included a new set of stabilizing jacks to give the launcher greater rigidity during launching, and folding platforms at the rear to assist the crew in reaching the launcher controls.

This side view of the 2P16 clearly shows the use of the distinctive PT-76 light amphibious tank chassis. A wheeled launcher vehicle, the 2P21 was also developed for this family but was not put into production.

The 2P16 Mars was widely used in the Warsaw Pact, in this case an East German NVA vehicle in Dresden showing the rear controls for the launcher. The rocket used a large solid fuel engine in the center, and a series of small venturis on the outer ring which gave the rocket the spin needed for stability. (Michael Jerchel)

The 2P16 used artillery controls similar to those in a conventional towed gun or multiple rocket launcher. Since there was no guidance on the rocket, initial positioning of the vehicle was critical. (Michael Jerchel)

The other rocket used with the 2K6 Luna series was the 3R-10, called FROG-3 in the West. This rocket used an enlarged warhead covering for its 3N14 nuclear warhead. This enlarged warhead had electrical coils to maintain the nuclear warhead temperature. This is a 2P16 on parade in the Soviet Union.

A 3R-10 rocket on a 2P16 TEL during summer exercises in the Soviet Union in the 1960s shows the enlarged tactical nuclear warhead of this type. In fact, this would be a dummy training round as tactical nuclear warheads were not fitted during exercises.

The FROG-6 was not a tactical rocket launcher after all, but merely a training device. These trainers, based on a ZIL-151 truck, were designed to acquaint new crews with the basic launch preparation drill.

Tactical nuclear rockets were issued to the Warsaw Pact forces starting in the early 1960s as part of the "revolution in military affairs". But the actual nuclear warheads were kept in Soviet custody at special bases. This is a Romanian 2P16 with the nuclear capable 3R-10 rocket with 3N14 warhead on parade in the 1970s in Bucharest, Romania.

The Luna-M (FROG-7) rocket appeared in 1965 and became the most common type of Soviet divisional nuclear artillery rocket system. This particular example is an Egyptian Luna-M; the Egyptians first used the FROG-7 in the 1973 war. (via J. Bermudez)

A Soviet Luna-M passes through a Czech town during summer wargames. The Luna-M originally used the 3R-11 rocket, also known as the R-65 and FROG-7a. But this type was uncommon, and quickly replaced by the more successful R-70 (FROG-7b).

An overhead view of a pair of Luna-M 9P113 TELs during a parade. The marking on the sides of the cab door is the Guards division honorific emblem. The 9M113 TEL was based on the ZIL-135LTM, later being renamed the BAZ-135LTM when production shifted to Briansk Automotive Plant (BAZ) in the 1970s.

An overhead view of a 9P113 Luna-M launch vehicle during the 1968 October Revolution parade in Moscow. For the Moscow parades, the vehicle is painted with white trim. The use of the red star on the cab door is usually only seen during parades, not during tactical use of the vehicle. The rocket itself is usually painted in a dull aluminum color to better reflect sunlight and prevent the internal rocket components from becoming overheated.

A right side view of an East German 9P113 launcher vehicle. The 9P113 incorporates a hydraulic crane on the right side which allows it to load itself.

An interesting close-up of a Luna-M rocket warhead. The R-70 rocket is also known by its industrial index number 9M21. The 9M21 rocket comes in four combat types: the 9M21F with a 9N18F HE-Frag warhead; the 9M21E with the 9N18E submunitions warhead; the 9M21B with the AA22 nuclear warhead; and the 9M21 Kh with a chemical warhead filled with VX agent. Besides the tactical rockets, crews often use the PV-65, which is a training round.

A Luna-M crew, an officer and three enlisted men, during training. Notice that the blast shield has been erected over the vehicle windshield to prevent damage during launching. (Sovfoto)

A pair of Luna-M during firing exercises. The vehicle in the foreground has speed brakes bolted to the rear. These slow the missile and permit it to be fired at targets closer to the launcher than is the case with unmodified rockets. (Sovfoto)

A Luna-M launch battery on field exercise. Soviet tank and motor rifle divisions were equipped with a Luna-M battalion consisting of two launch batteries, each battery with two 9P113 launch vehicles. (Sovfoto)

A Luna-M launch battery ready to fire. Note that there are four stabilizing jacks on the 9P113 TEL, a pair behind the front axle and another pair at the rear. (Sovfoto)

A 9P113 Luna-M launcher of the Soviet Army in temporary winter whitewash camouflage.

An exceptionally gaudy paint scheme on a 9P113 Luna-M launch vehicle. The soldier standing on the vehicle crane has his right hand in the orifice of the spin-stabilizing vernier. When the rocket is launched, this vernier and the other like it around the circumference of the rocket are ignited, causing the rocket to spin. This spin-stabilization is the only form of guidance the rocket has. (Sovfoto)

The same Luna-M launch battery in their parade finish. The insignia on the cab door is for the Order of the Red Banner. Also worth noting is the windshield blast panel, locked in its protective position. (Sovfoto)

When the 9M21 rocket is being prepared for launch, a pair of platforms on either side are lowered to allow the crew easier access to the sighting and aligning equipment at the rear of the launch station.

An overhead view of a snow-covered 9P113 launch vehicle during one of the periodic Moscow Red Square parades. The 9M21 rocket is locked to the launcher with two straps during transit. Almost certainly this is a practice rocket rather than a tactical round.

An overhead view of a 9P113 launcher vehicle. The 9P113 designation for the BAZ-135LTM vehicle has the following meaning: 9= tactical missile; P= puskovaya ustanovka (launch system) and 113 is the numerical sequence of this particular launch vehicle. The two vertical fins evident midway down the rocket fuselage are intended to keep the rocket firmly on track when fired from the launch rail.

A right side view of a German 9P113 launcher vehicle in travel mode with the rear stabilizing pads folded up.

A left side view of a Soviet 9P113 launcher vehicle. Careful comparison with the photo of the German 9P113 will show what appears to be detail differences between the stabilizing pads. In fact, this view shows the top of the pads, rather than the bottom of the pads due to a different method of locking down the pads during travel.

The ZiL-135 truck on which the 9P113 is based has an unusual propulsion system: it has two ZIL-135 engines, behind the cab on either side of the vehicle.

An overall view of the sighting and aligning equipment on the left side of the Luna-M launcher.

A detailed rear view of an Iraqi 9P113 shipped to the US after Desert Storm. (Stephen Sewell)

Once the rocket is prepared for firing the crew sets up a launch station some distance from the 9P113. This East German crew has a theodolite between them, and the launch control box in front of them.

A number of Iraqi 9P113 Luna-M (FROG-7) rocket launchers were captured during Operation Desert Storm, in this case a vehicle captured by the US Marine Corps in Kuwait. (USMC)

A detail close-up shot of the hydraulic crane on the right side of the vehicle.

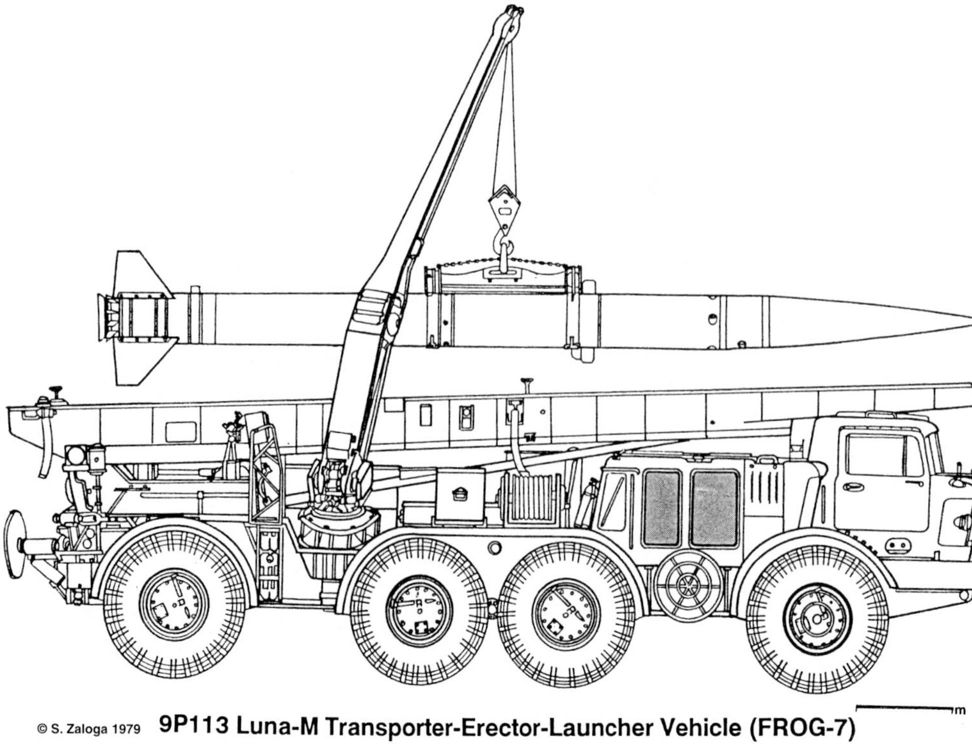

m

© S. Zaloga 1979 **9P113 Luna-M Transporter-Erector-Launcher Vehicle (FROG-7)**

A detail view of a training 9M21 (FROG-7) rocket showing the speed brakes added when the crew wished to fire at a shorter-range target. This example is preserved at the Buck Technologies museum in Pinnow, Germany where many of these rockets were de-militarized.

A 9P113 (FROG-7) launcher vehicle of the German NVA during the annual parade in Berlin in the 1980s.

A view of the right side of a 9P113 launcher vehicle (FROG-7) of the German NVA in Berlin in the late 1980s prior to the German reunification.

The 9T29 is a transloader vehicle for the Luna-M firing battery. It carries up to three additional 9M21 rockets for the FROG-7 divisional rocket system. This is an East German vehicle on parade in Berlin in 1974.

The 9T29 transloader vehicle is based on the same ZIL-135/BAZ-135 chassis as the 9P113 launcher vehicle. This head-on view of the 9T29 transloader vehicle is in East German service.

A rear view of an East German 9T29 transloader vehicle during a parade in Berlin in 1974.

An East German 9T29 transloader on parade in Berlin. The transloader, unlike the 9P113 TEL, did not have a crane for loading the missiles.

A rear view of the 9T29 transloader vehicle showing the three 9M21 rockets.

One of the principal problems with the 9P113 launch vehicle is that it leaves the rocket exposed on the launch rail. In the mid-1960s, the Soviets experimented with a modified 9P113 launch vehicle enclosed in an environmental shelter. Although deployed for a time in East Germany, this system was never put into widespread operational use.

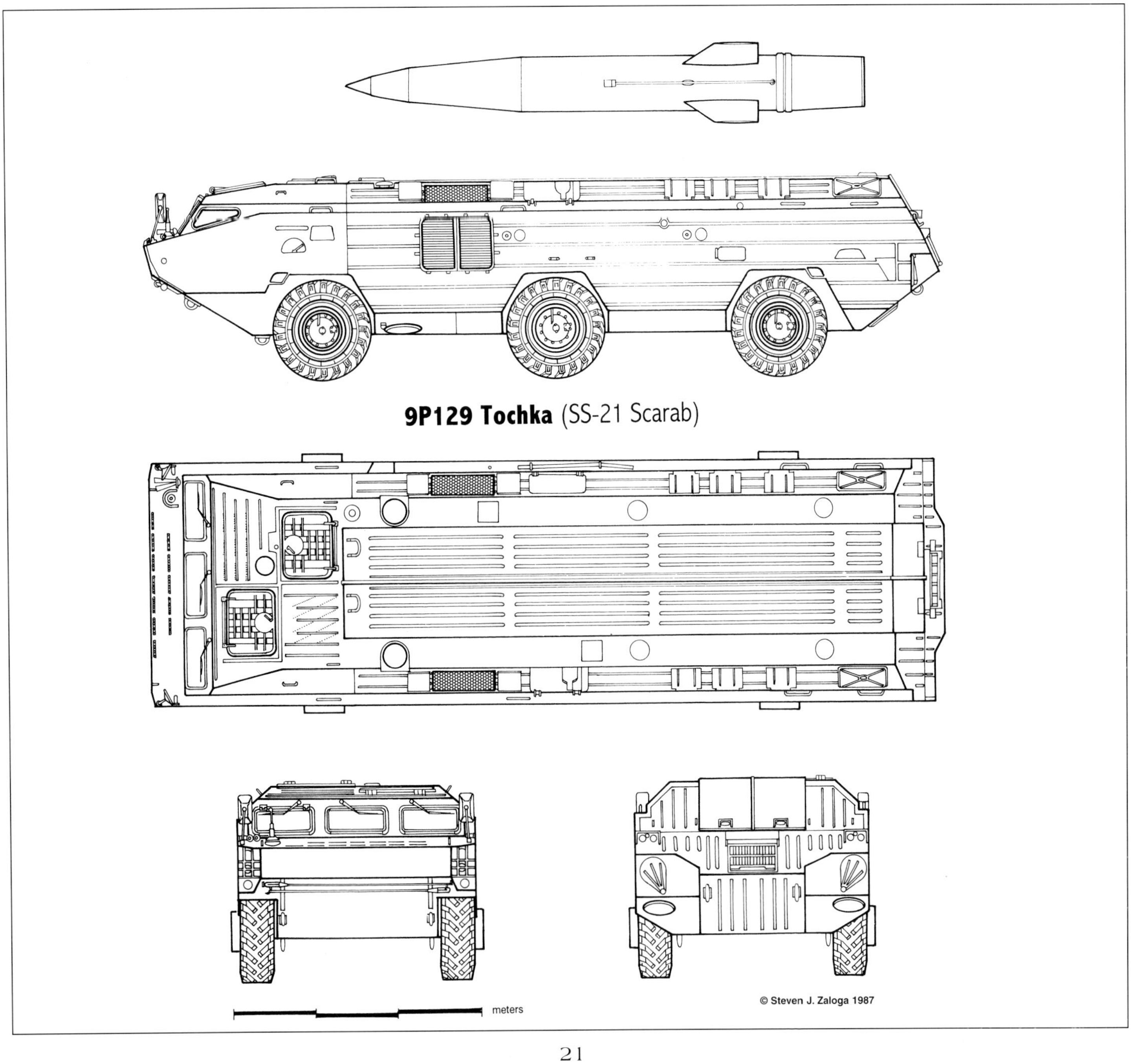

9P129 Tochka (SS-21 Scarab)

meters

In the 1980s, select divisions began to have their Luna-M rocket launchers replaced by the vastly improved 9K79 Tochka (Point; NATO: SS-21 Scarab) ballistic missile. This 9P129 launcher carries the missile completely under cover until launch. In this view of a vehicle on parade, the launcher is only partially raised. It would be raised to the near vertical position to actually launch the 9M79 missile.

A view of the left side of the 9P129 Tochka launcher vehicle. The vehicle is based on the BAZ-5921 chassis, a relative of the vehicle used with the SA-8 Gecko (Osa-M) air defense missile system.

This view of a Czechoslovak 9P129 Tochka launcher vehicle in Prague in 1985 shows it in the more typical travel mode with the missile completely enclosed within the vehicle.

A pair of 9P129 Tochka launchers on parade in the USSR with the missiles partly elevated for display.

An excellent side view of the 9P129 Tochka-U launcher with the missile elevated to the launch position. The Tochka-U is an improved, longer-ranged version of the missile.

An interesting forward view of the 9P129 Tochka-U that shows the configuration of the launch rail for the missile.

A 9P129 Tochka-U system on display in Nizhni-Novgorod in the mid-1990s. This employs a three tone camouflage scheme of sand-gray and black over the usual dark green camouflage.

Another view of the Tochka-U system on display in Nizhni-Novgorod. Careful inspection of the photo will show that the centerline stabilizing jacks are in the extended position.

A 9P129 Tochka-U on display in the United Arab Emirates in the early 1990s. This is in a desert camouflage scheme of sand over the usual dark green. (Christopher Foss)

A nice view of the 9P129 Tochka-U from the left side showing the desert camouflage scheme used during demonstrations in the UAE. (Christopher Foss)

A rear view of a Soviet 9P129 launcher vehicle. When ready for firing, the launcher rail is erected to the near vertical position through the opening in the rear of the chassis. There are four stabilization pads on the vehicle: a pair behind the first axle and another pair on the hull rear behind the third axle. The unusual grid vanes on the rear of the 9M79 missile are an advanced alternative to more conventional fins called Belotserkovskiy grid fins.

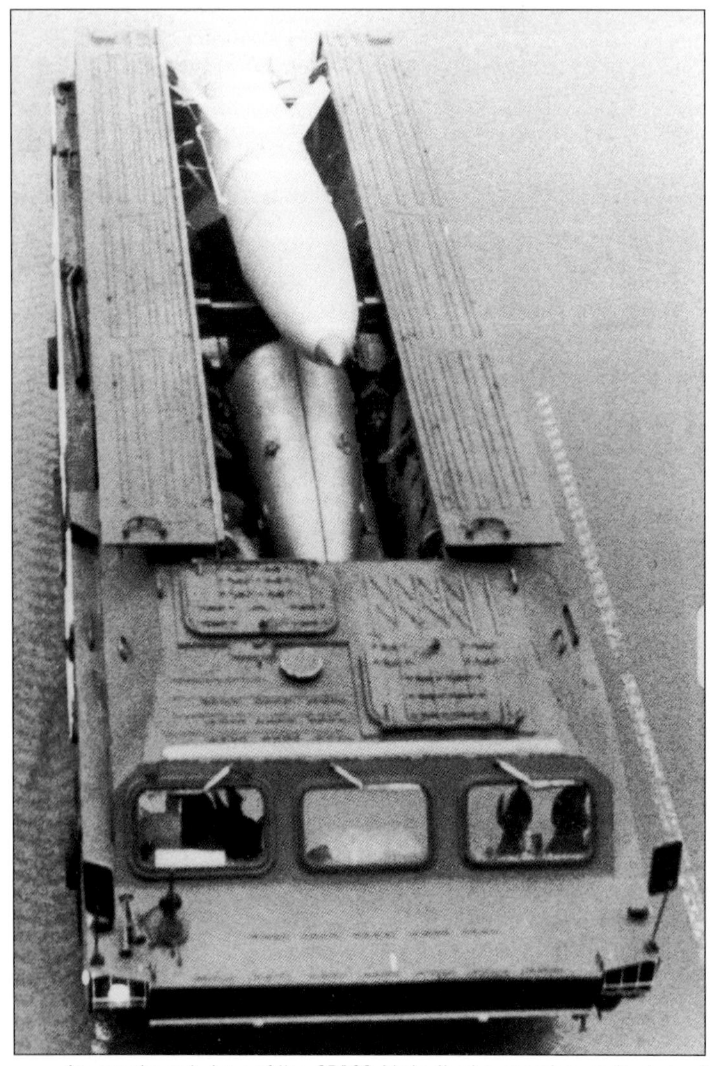

An overhead view of the 9P129. Note that a crossbeam is placed into the compartment to keep the missile locked in a semi-raised position during the parade. The normal elevating system for the missile is not designed to keep the heavy missile in a semi-raised position for prolonged periods of time- hence the improvised alteration.

A view of the Tochka-U missile in firing position with the stabilizing jacks extended and the Belotserkovskiy fins fully extended.

An excellent overhead view of the 9P129 launcher vehicle. The BAZ-5921 chassis on which the 9P129 is based is powered by the 5D20B engine - the same type used in the BMP-1 infantry combat vehicle. The four man crew sits in the completely enclosed forward cab, which can be sealed against chemical agents. The large structure under the missile is the warhead cover which can be used to stabilize the temperature of the warhead during transit. Certain warheads, such as the AA60 nuclear warhead on the 9M79B missile need careful temperature control for proper functioning.

A view down into the compartment showing details of the interior. The stenciling on the missile warhead identifies it as the 9N123K-UT training warhead. (Christopher Foss)

A rear view of the 9P129 Tochka-U showing the improved 9K79M-1 Tochka-U missile erected for launch. This shows the markings used on actual combat missiles. The many stripes around the missile are used to help line up the missile on the launcher.

Although similar in appearance to the 9P129 launcher vehicle, the 9T218 transloader vehicle is designed to reload the launcher vehicle. It carries two reload missiles in the rear compartment along with a crane for lifting the missiles.

The earliest model of the Scud, the R-11 missile, was mounted on a modified ISU-152 heavy assault gun chassis called the 8U218 TEL. It was reminiscent of the similar Filin/FROG-1 launcher seen earlier in this book. The 8U218 launcher vehicle can be distinguished from the later 2P19 version by the presence of one high pressure air bottle on the hull superstructure- the later 2P19 version had two bottles on either side. This is a Polish LWP 8U218 launcher vehicle. There is a thermal blanket over the warhead to maintain temperature.

A pair of East German NVA 8U218 TEL (SS-1b Scud A) of the Lenkflugkorpferbrigade "Otto Shwab", normally stationed at Hermsdorf with the 3.NVA-Armee. These vehicles remained in service into the 1970s, some of the last vehicles based on the ISU-152 assault gun to survive so long in service.

A Czechoslovak CSLA 8U218 TEL. This version of the Scud missile, the Scud A (R-11) was shorter than the more familiar Scud B used during the Gulf War. The Czechoslovak Army had three R-11 brigades, numbering about 36 launchers.

A Romanian ASR 8U218 TEL missile launcher on parade in Bucharest. The Romanians had two R-11 brigades, the 32nd and 37th Operational-Tactical Missile Brigades with the 2nd Army at Tecuci and the 3rd Army at Ineu, using them well into the 1980s due to a lack of more modern equipment.

An overhead view of a Polish 8K11 (Scud A) launcher vehicle. The basic launcher configuration has certain clear similarities to the later 9P117 launcher vehicle, especially the base plate/deflector.

A parade of Polish LWP 8K11 missile launchers in Warsaw in the 1960s. The 8K11 was the only version of the tracked Scud launcher commonly exported to the Warsaw Pact. Poland had a total of four brigades of these, each with about 12 launchers.

Hungarian 8U218 TELs of the only Hungarian Scud unit, the 5th Ind. Mixed Tapolca Missile Brigade, during a parade in Budapest in the early 1970s.

A close-up rear-view of the right side of a German 8U218 TEL showing the trunnion and elevation mechanism of the launcher.

A Polish 8K11 launcher vehicle in the field in the 1960s. The elaborate bracing around the missile was designed in part to protect it against damage, but also permit launch crews to climb up alongside the missile to check various features prior to launch.

A Polish 8U218 TEL preserved outside of Warsaw. The device on the front fender is a folding ladder which the crew could use to get on and off the vehicle.

Another view of a Polish 8U218 TEL from the left side showing the launch cab area. The driver was seated quite low in the hull, and used the small oval window at the bottom of the door.

A view of the left rear of the 8U218 TEL showing the trunnion area and elevating mechanisms.

A view of the right rear of a Polish 8U218 TEL showing the baseplate, elevating mechanism and other details.

A rear view of a Polish 8U218 TEL showing the baseplate. This launch pad would be elevated to the ground prior to firing.

A view over the top of the 8U218 TEL showing the missile and the top of the overhead compartments.

A view over the top of a Polish 8U218 TEL towards the front showing the elaborate brush guard in front of the missile.

The 8U218 TEL was succeeded by the very similar 2P19. The 2P19 used the new R-17 missile, known to NATO as the SS-1c Scud B. The R-17 missile was longer than the R-11, requiring a reconfigured launcher. The modified 2P19 launcher can be most easily distinguished by the two high pressure air bottles on either side of the vehicle superstructure, as well as by the more elaborate reinforcing frame on the front of the hull.

A firing battery of Soviet 2P19 (Scud B) launchers in the field. From this angle, it is very hard to distinguish the 2P19 from the earlier 8U218 TEL, except by careful inspection of the heavier reinforcement on the hull front.

2P4 Filin (FROG-1) tactical ballistic rocket launcher, Soviet Army, 1957

The Filin launcher was built in very small numbers and was so secret at the time, that it was very plainly marked when in service. The basic scheme is overall Soviet olive green. The missile was painted in aluminum for training missiles, and olive green for tactical missiles.

2P6 Luna (FROG-3) tactical ballistic rocket launcher, Polish People's Army, 1960

The Polish People's Army followed Soviet camouflage practices and finished their Luna launcher vehicles in an olive green shade about the same as the Soviet pattern. The Polish national insignia from 1943 through the 1960s was the white Piast Eagle, later switched to the red-and-white "szachownica" checkerboard diamond in the 1970s.

9P113 Luna-M (FROG-7) tactical ballistic rocket launcher, Soviet Army, 1970

The Soviet Army occasionally camouflage painted its equipment with whitewash during winter wargames. This was a temporary paint that was usually washed off after the exercise. This vehicle carries a tactical number "01" on the door in the standard white color.

9T29 rocket transloader vehicle, German People's Army, 1980

The East German Army painted their equipment in a gray-green color that was somewhat lighter and grayer than the color used on other Warsaw Pact equipment. This is a vehicle in parade markings with the DDR roundel on the cab door and on the rockets. The rockets were usually finished in gray and aluminum paint for parades.

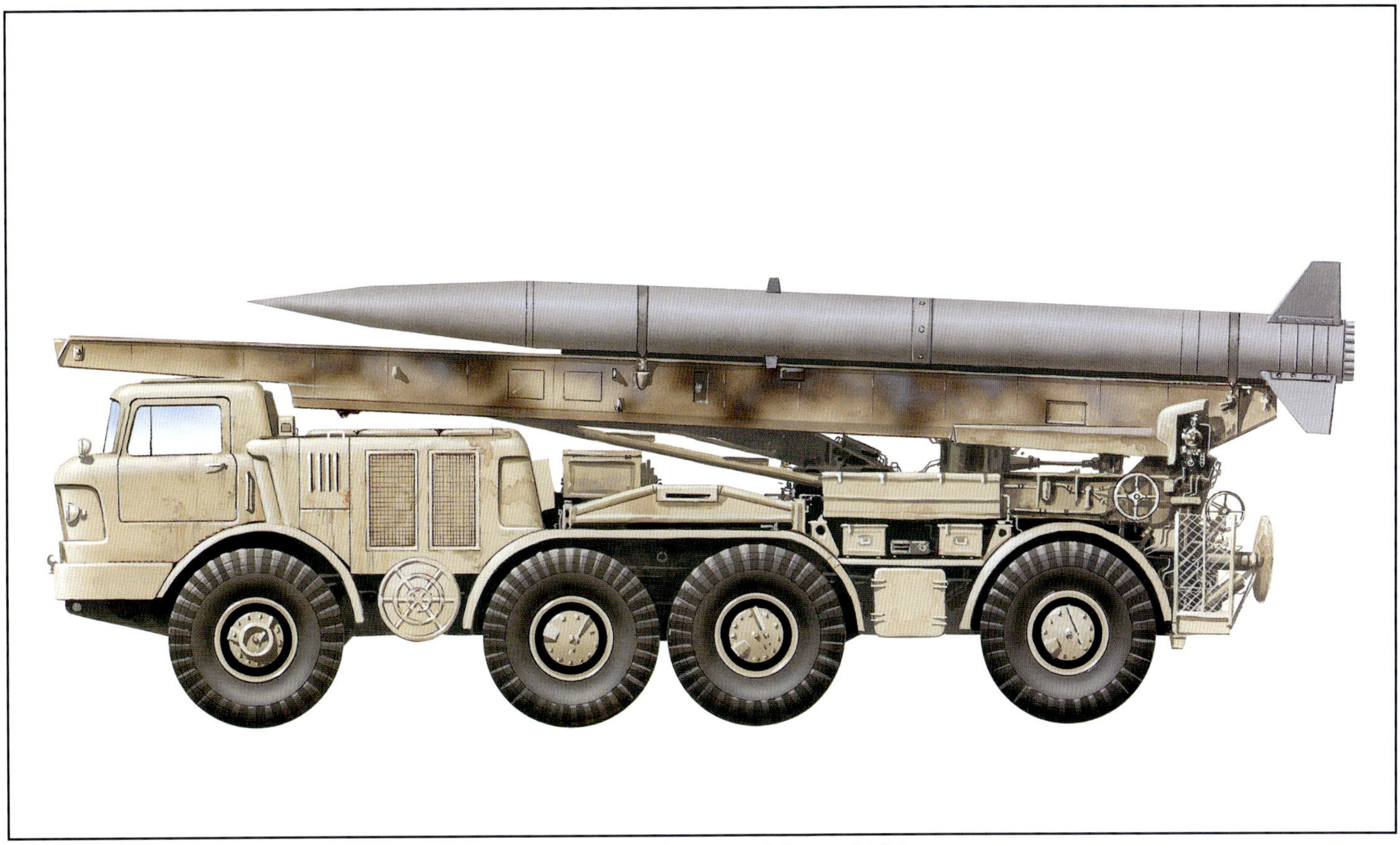

9P113 Luna-M (FROG-7) tactical ballistic rocket launcher, Iraqi Army, 1991

Iraqi Luna-M launchers were usually finished in a pale stone color, sometimes with a light overspray pattern of a slightly darker pale brown. The Iraqi Scud launchers were in a similar finish.

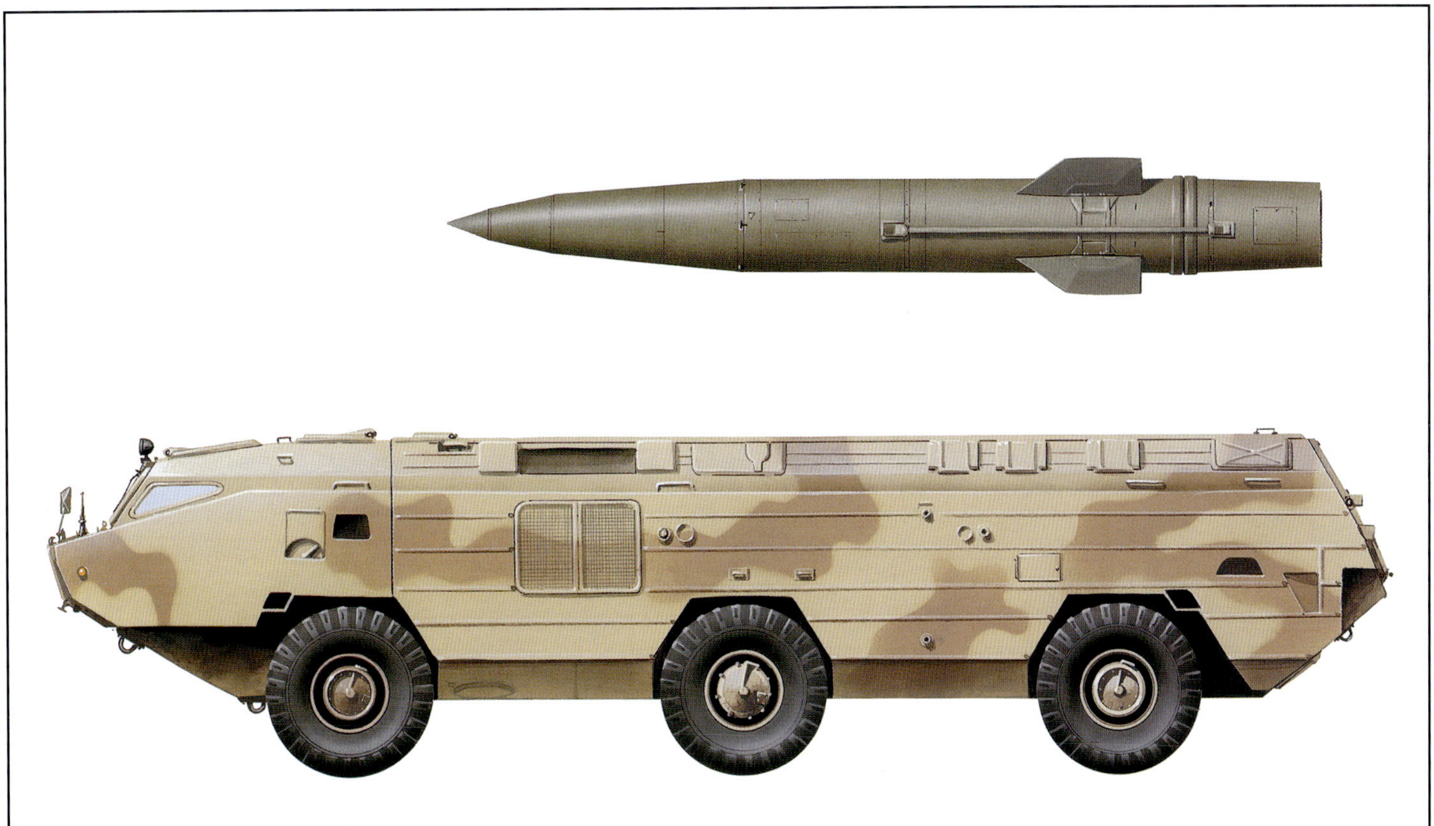

9P129 Tochka (SS-21 Scarab) tactical ballistic missile launcher, UAE, 1993

While Russian Tochka launchers are finished in the usual temperate patterns, this Tochka launcher was camouflaged in desert colors for an exhibition in the United Arab Emirates in 1993. The scheme was pale brown over a pale stone color. The missile itself is finished in the usual olive green, except for display and training missiles which are often in aluminum color.

8U218 (SS-1b Scud A) operational-tactical ballistic missile launcher, Polish People's Army, 1960

Polish Scud launchers were finished in the normal Warsaw Pact dark olive green. These early launchers carried the white Piast Eagle national insignia, and there is a small tactical insignia painted on the right co-driver's window. The missile had an extensive pattern of markings, most of them white bands used when loading the missile by crane on to the launcher to indicate the location of the reinforced missile frames.

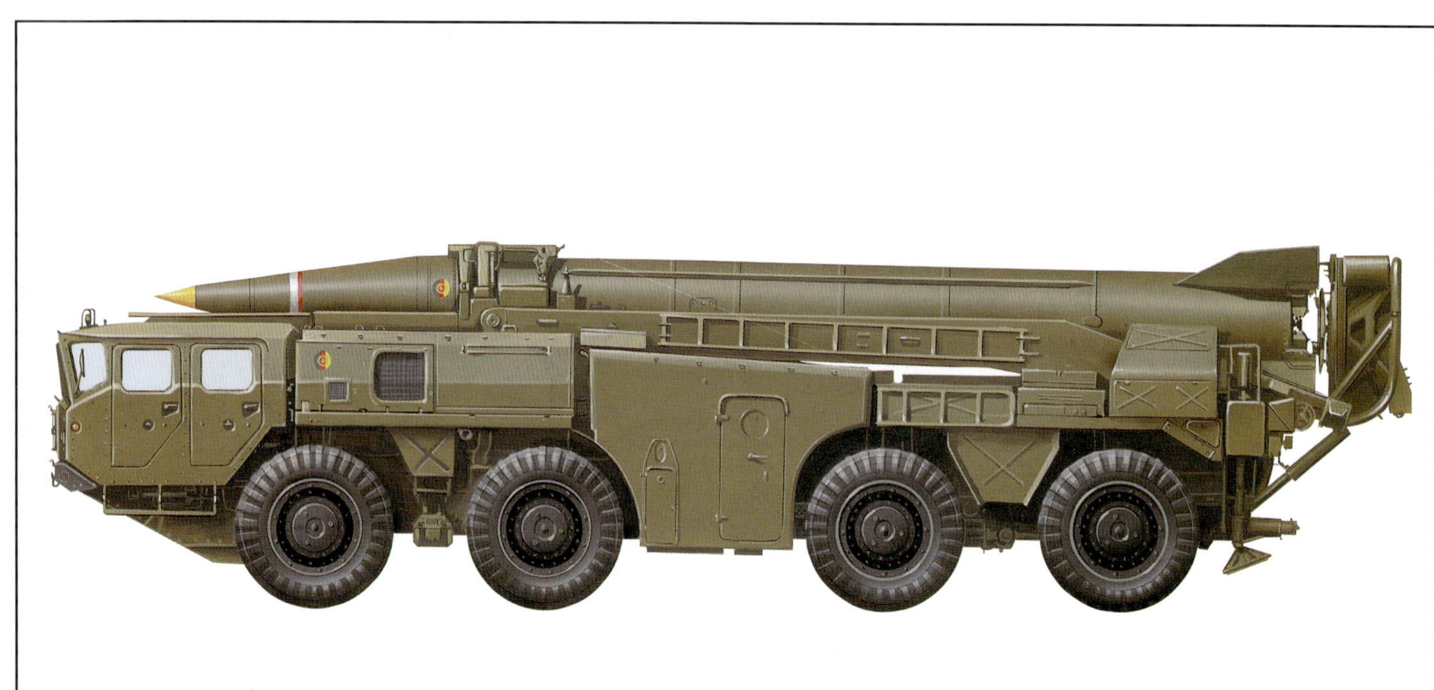

9P117M (SS-1c Scud B) operational-tactical missile launcher, Otto Schwab Brigade, German People's Army, 1985

East German Scud launchers were painted in a gray-green color like other NVA equipment. The chassis frame was painted in semi-gloss black as were the wheel hubs. This is a parade finish, as the missile lacks the full set of loading markings.

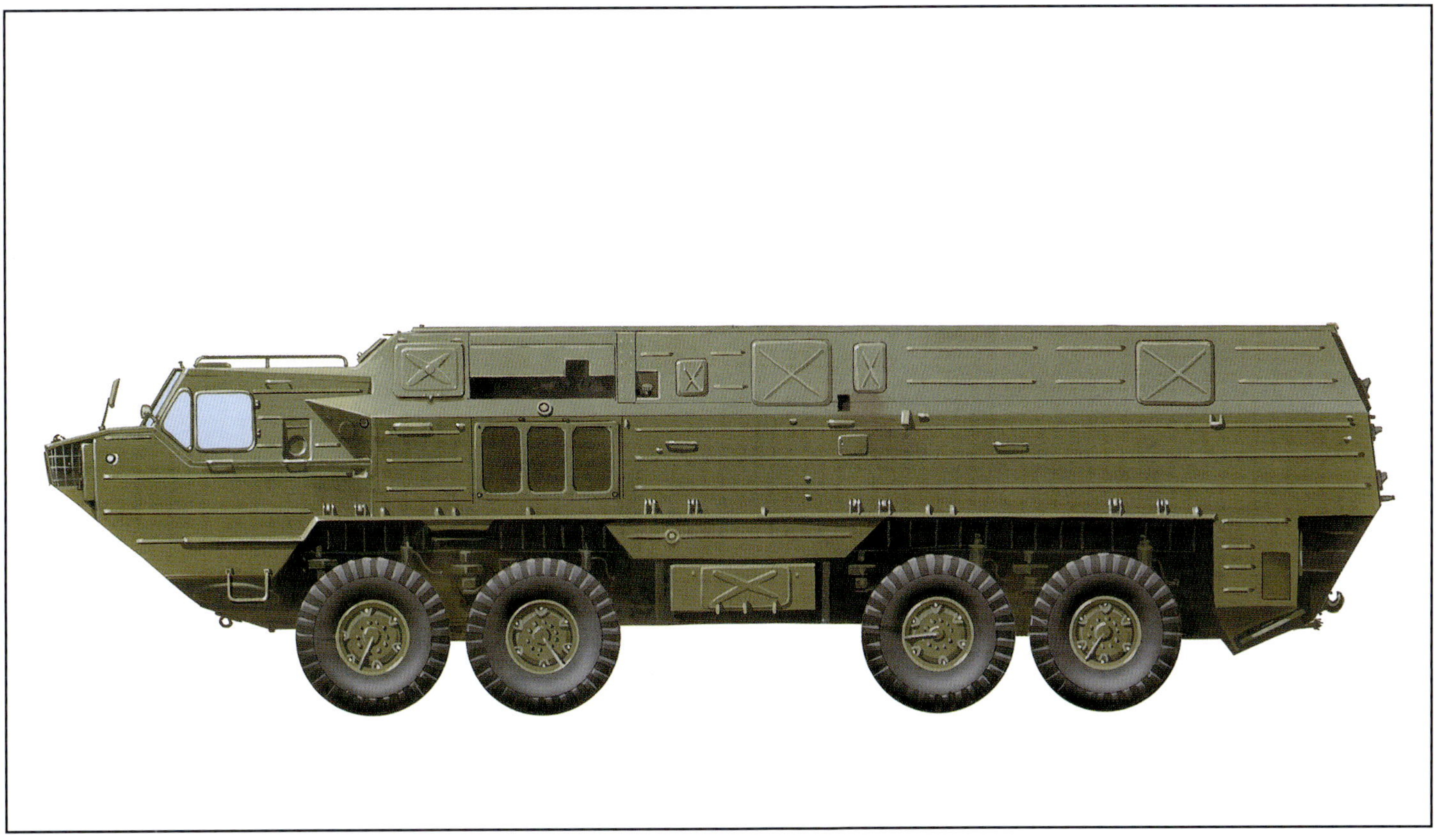

9P71 Oka (SS-23 Spider) operational-tactical missile launcher, Soviet Army, 1985

When first deployed in the 1980s, the Okas were considered very secret and were very plainly marked in overall dark olive green. They were dismantled under the terms of the 1987 INF treaty, and so had largely disappeared before the more colorful three-color camouflage scheme appeared.

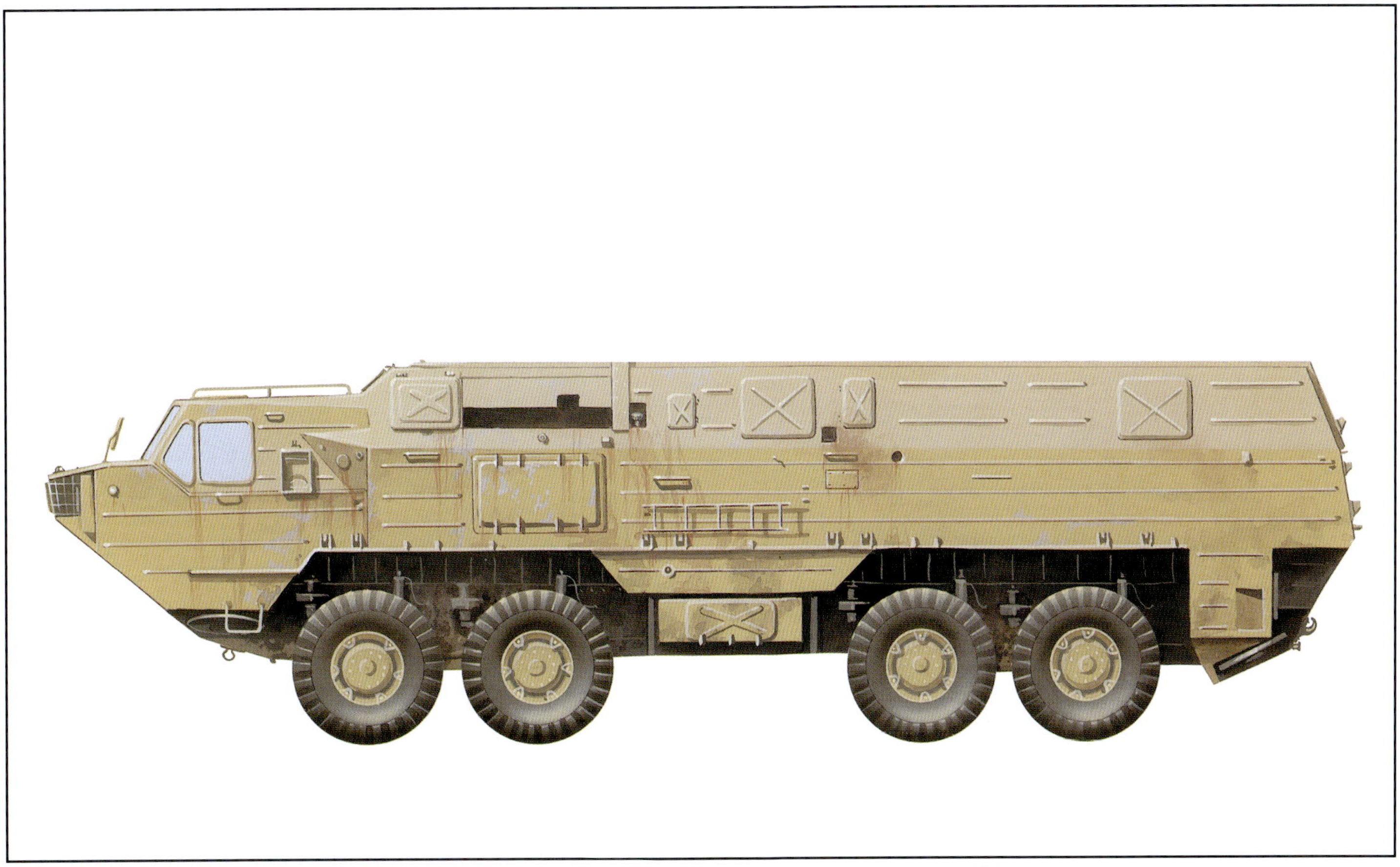

9P71 Oka (SS-23 Spider) operational-tactical missile launcher, Export variant, 1985

There were plans to export the Oka as a replacement for the Scud before the INF treaty intervened. This is an Oka launcher in the usual plain stone color for Mid-East export.

9P120 Temp-S (SS-12 Scaleboard) operational ballistic missile launcher, Soviet Army, 1985

The Temp-S was usually marked in a very simple fashion when in combat service. During parades after Warsaw Pact wargames, they would occasionally be brightened up with a red star, but this was not a normal tactical marking.

SPU-35V Redut (SSC-1b Shaddock), Soviet Navy Coastal Missile Battery, 1985

Soviet Navy coastal launchers were plainly finished in the usual dark olive green color. They often carried white tactical numbers on the cab side that were probably related to their registration number for maintenance purposes, rather than to their unit function.

3P51 Rubezh (SSC-3 Styx), German People's Navy KRR 18 "Waldemar Verner", 1985

Rubezh launchers of the German Navy were painted in the same gray-green color as army vehicles, and also had the chassis painted in semi-gloss black like the Scud launchers. The naval missile regiments sometimes carried a navy anchor tactical sign in yellow on the side of the operators' shelter.

SM-SP21 (SS-15 Scrooge) strategic missile launcher, Soviet RVSN, 1968

The Scrooge never saw actual deployment, but was a popular fixture at Moscow May Day Parades. As a result, it was seen most often in parade markings with white trim and red stars over the usual dark olive green finish.

15P72 Pioner (SS-20 Saber) strategic missile launcher, Soviet RVSN, 1985

The Pioner was not usually camouflage pattern painted in service, relying instead on a large camouflage net as seen here. As was common with most truck-based missile launchers, the chassis was finished in gloss black, while the superstructure was in the usual dark olive green.

RT-2PM Topol (SS-25 Sickle) strategic missile launcher, Russian RVSN, 1995

In the late 1980s, NII Stadi developed a three-color camouflage pattern reminiscent of the US Army MERDC scheme. The three colors in this pattern are dark olive green (*zeleno-zashchitniy*), yellow-gray (*sero-zheltiy*), and black (*cherniy*). Most Russian mobile strategic missile launchers are now painted in this or other camouflage schemes.

A Soviet 2P19 with the missile being elevated, showing the launch cradle details. The 2P19 was not commonly exported, most countries waiting for the later 9P117M launcher to become available. This view shows the heavier reinforcing cradle on the hull front.

In 1965, the new 9P117 launcher vehicle became available. This fired the same R-17 missile as the earlier 2P19 launcher on the ISU-152 assault gun chassis but from a new system mounted on a MAZ-543 heavy truck. The initial 9P117 series had a heavy frame for the launcher which enable it to reload missiles from the transloader without use of a crane. The basic 9P117 version can be distinguished by the large box structures on either side of the launcher frame, seen clearly here along the mid-section of the R-17 missile.

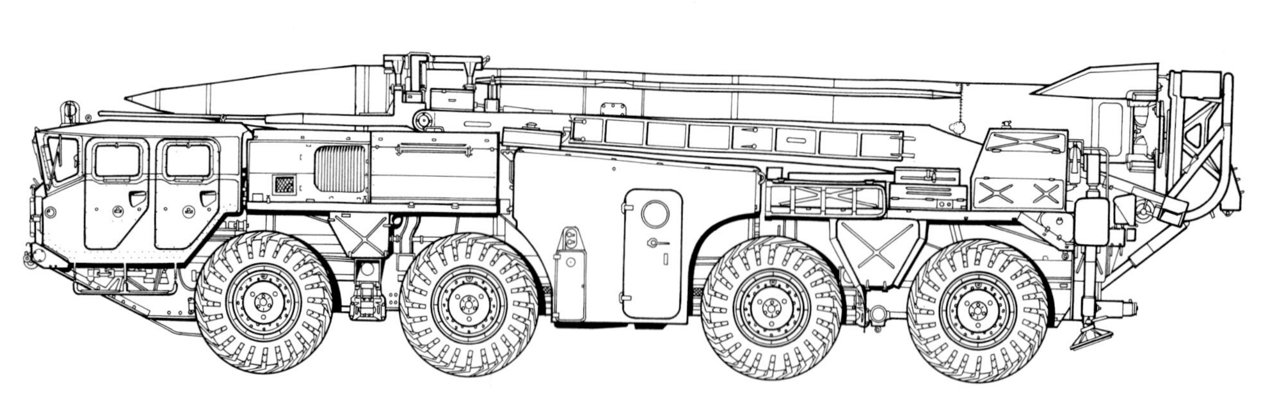

9P117 Elbrus (SS-1c Scud B)

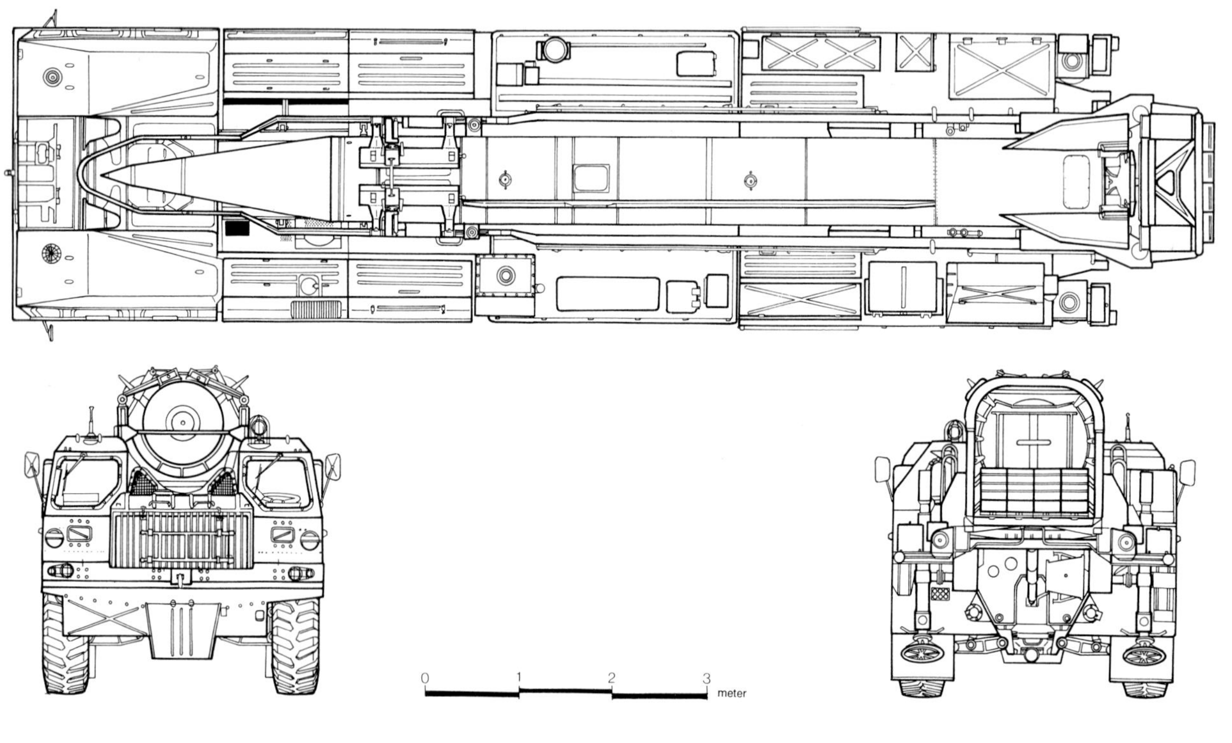

There are at least three production versions of the 9P117 TEL. On this intermediate version, there are no vents on the compartment over the first wheel.

On the final production variant of the 9P117, there is a row of vents on the compartment side over the first wheel, identical to the panel and early and intermediate production 9P117Ms.

An overhead view of an intermediate production 9P117. This view more clearly shows the hydraulic cylinders on the missile launcher cradle characteristic of this family of TELs as well as the box structure on the side of the launcher frame.

An overhead view of the 9P117 currently preserved at the Polish Army Museum in Warsaw. At the extreme left of the picture, the characteristic hydraulic cylinders of this version are evident. (Frank DeSisto)

The early production 9P117 had three portholes on the left compartment side, as is evident on this Polish 9P117. Also worth noting is the 2Sh2 thermal blanket over the warhead section. This is used to stabilize the warhead temperature when using "special" warheads, such as the Type 269A nuclear warhead.

A Polish 9P117 launcher with the missile fully erected. This gives some idea of the greater complexity of the launcher cradle on this family of TELs. The left central compartment of the launcher vehicle contains missile checking equipment to determine proper fuel level, battery status and other features necessary in preparing the missile for launch.

The 9P117 was built in parallel to a less expensive version of the basic TEL called the 9P117. This version was essentially similar to the basic 9P117 but lacked the self-loading equipment on the launcher frame. Note the lack of the box structure and hydraulic cylinders on the missile launcher frame. As in the case of the 9P117 series, the 9P117M series under went production changes during its manufacture. The initial production version of the 9P117M can be distinguished by the three portholes on the left crew servicing compartment at the center of the vehicle. This is a German 9P117M.

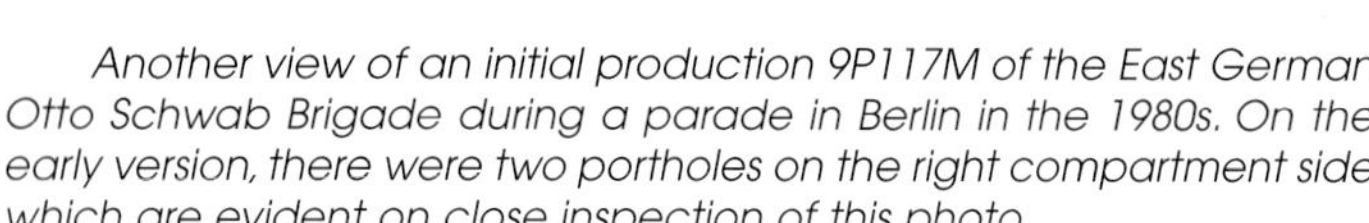

Another view of an initial production 9P117M of the East German Otto Schwab Brigade during a parade in Berlin in the 1980s. On the early version, there were two portholes on the right compartment side which are evident on close inspection of this photo.

The second production variant of the 9P117M launcher vehicle had only a single porthole on the left compartment door, compared to three on the first production version. This is more clearly evident on the Soviet 9P117M in the background than the foreground vehicle.

An overhead view of a Soviet 9P117M of the second production batch on parade in 1990 showing overhead details of the center section.

A right side view of a Soviet second production batch 9P117M. Note that there is only one porthole in the door (the other circular opening does not have a transparent opening). This shows the standard 7 man crew: a launch section commander, a warrant officer for aiming the missile, a warrant officer missile preparation checks, a sergeant who drives the 9P117M and three enlisted men who do the dirty work.

A view of a pair of 9P117 launch vehicles. The vehicle in the foreground is the 9P117 evident from its less elaborate launcher frame compared to the vehicle in the background which is a 9P117 with the more elaborate launcher frame.

An overhead view of a standard second production variant 9P117M. Note the presence of only one porthole on the central compartment side. The right side compartment contains the ballistic computation equipment for preparing firing data for the missile.

A detail side view of the 9P117M launcher showing the right side of the vehicle work cab on an East German launcher.

A view of the rear baseplate on a 9P117M from a slightly different angle showing some of the rear detail to better effect.

A left side view of the third and final production variant, the 9P117M1. This version can be distinguished by the different side exhaust panel behind the crew cab. On the two earlier versions, the panel had small vertical vents, on this version, there is a large screen vent. This difference was due to the fact that the early versions used an APD-8-P/28-2 auxiliary power unit with a Pobeda radiator, while the 9P117M1 used the -2M version of the unit with a GAZ-69 radiator Otherwise, the launchers are very similar. This is the version of the 9P117 represented in the 1/35 scale Dragon (DML) kit.

An example of the final production type 9P117M1 in Soviet service. In the field, the 9P117 vehicles are very simply marked with tactical numbers and lack the elaborate white pin-stripes, Guards markings and other decorations found on parade vehicles.

A side view of a 9P117M1 launcher vehicle of the third and final production type. The 9P117M is officially called Uragan (Hurricane), but its Russian crews usually call it the Kashalot (Sperm Whale) due to its enormous size.

An overhead view of the 9P117 cab showing many details. The vehicle radio is located in the right cab, the driver in the left.

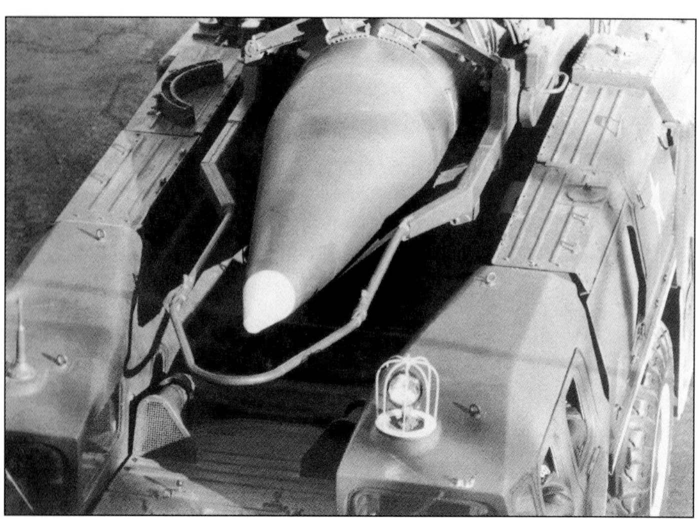

An overhead view of a 9P117M showing a closeup of the missile warhead. The forward tip of the warhead contains the fuze, often a proximity fuze for airburst. The R-17 can be fitted with nuclear, chemical or high explosive warheads.

An overhead view of the cradle which holds the missile in place during transit and while the missile is being erected. The basic cradle assembly on the 9P117 is the same as on the 9P117M, but there are additional cradle elements stowed on the compartment roofs which are peculiar to the 9P117 version. Further to the rear, the distinctive hydraulic cylinders of this variant are evident.

A detail view looking into the cavity under the missile cradle.

A view under the missile showing the hydraulic cylinder used to lift the missile launcher. (Frank DeSisto)

An overhead view of a 9P117 in transit. The crew has a cold-weather cover over the engine radiator vent. This can be entirely closed off if the weather is cold enough to prevent the water in the radiator from freezing. (Sovfoto)

A 9P117M on parade in Moscow. On tactical vehicles, the bumper is usually painted black, along with much of the undersides of the vehicle.

A close-up view of the nose of a German 9P117M. Four of the seven crewmen sit in the two front cabs.

A detail shot of the area behind the left cab. The screen opening, the distinctive feature of the third and final production batch of the 9P117M1, is clearly evident here. This view also shows the cradle lock assembly that prevents the missile from moving about in the cradle during transit and erection.

A rear view of a Soviet 9P117M1 of the final production type showing rear details of the launcher base plate and deflector.

A German 9P117M of the initial production type with the two portholes on the right compartment side.

A detail view of a Scud baseplate, in this case however, a modified Iraqi launcher for the lengthened Al-Husayn missile. The baseplate is constructed to permit the missile to be carefully adjusted to true vertical position. (Christopher Foss)

An R-17 missile being prepared for firing. A large amount of cabling is required, some of which is used to pass ignition signals to engine components, other of which provides data back to the launch control station to monitor the status of the missile prior to launch.

The R-17 missile was redesignated as the R-300 in the 1980s. The export version is known as the R-17E or R-300E. Here an R-300 (SS-1c Scud B) is ready for launch. (Sovfoto)

A close-up view of an R-300 missile ready for launch. The compartment behind the warhead contains the missile's inertial guidance system. The nosecone of the missile is a dielectric material distinctly different in color from the rest of the missile since it contains a radar proximity fuze. (Sovfoto)

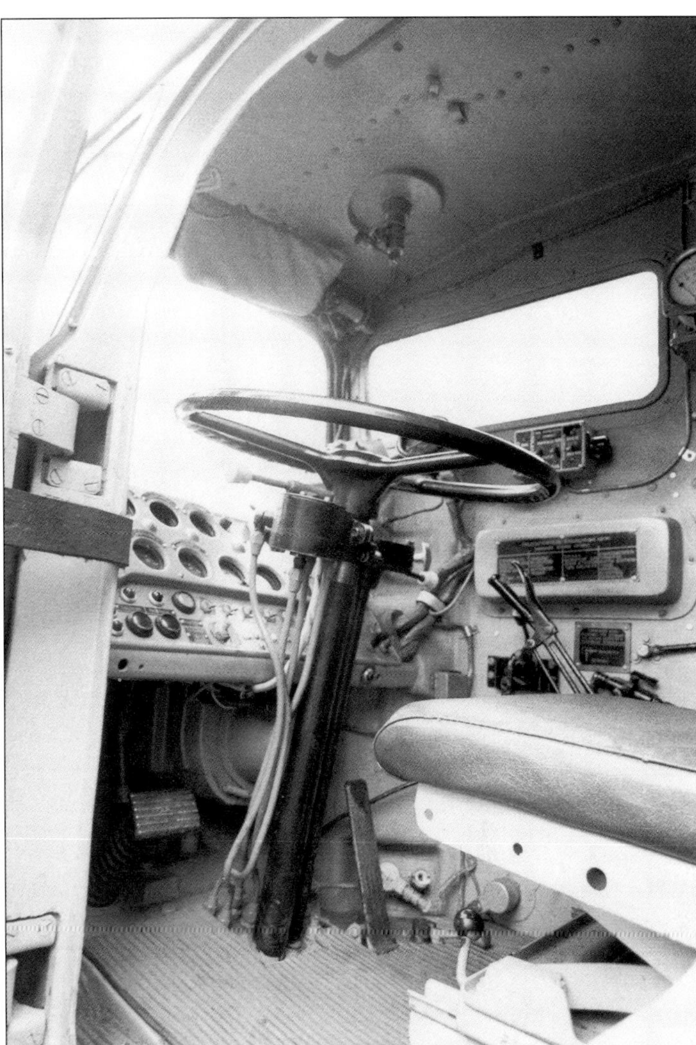

A view inside the cab of a 9P117 showing the steering wheel and other driver controls. (Frank DeSisto)

A close-up of an R-17 missile on a 2T3M semi-trailer, giving a good detail view of the rear of the missile and the graphite vanes used to steer the missile.

To transport the R-17 missile into the combat area, the 2T3M is used, which consists of a ZIL-157 truck towing a semi-trailer for the missile. Some units use the newer 2T3M1 combination which uses a ZIL-131 truck instead.

A 9P117M launcher vehicle (SS-1c Scud B) of the German Otto Schwab Brigade on parade in Berlin in the 1980s. Note the red curtains over the two porthole of the ballistic computation compartment. These portholes identify this particular launcher as being of the initial production type.

Another view of a German 9P117M (Scud) launcher vehicle of the Otto Schwab Brigade in Berlin in the 1980s.

An Iraqi Al-Husayn missile shot down by Patriot missiles during the Gulf War. The Al-Husayn was a modified R-300E (SS-1c Scud B) missile which had a reduced high explosive fill and lengthened fuel tanks to give it greater range than a normal Scud.

A detail shot of an Al-Husayn missile downed during the Gulf War by Patriots. The center section seen in this photo is one of two additional lengths of fuel tanks used to extend the Scud B missile for greater range. The dark circular pattern on the other sections resulted from the sand camouflage paint blistering from the heat during missile entry. The Al-Husayn was lengthened 1.3 meters (4' 3") compared to the normal Scud B.

The Oka (SS-23 Spider) was developed as a replacement for the 9K72 Elbrus (SS-1c Scud B). It entered service in small numbers after 1986, but soon afterwards was withdrawn and dismantled due to the range restrictions of the INF Treaty. This is the Oka's 9P71 launcher vehicle, based on the BAZ-6944. It resembles an enlarged 9P129 from the Tochka system since they were both designed by the same organization.

This is the 9P71 TEL with the missile stowed inside. Although similar in appearance to the 9P129 Tochka, it is in fact considerably larger. This is a retired Czechoslovak example. (Andrzej Kinski)

This could be mistaken for an 9P71 launcher vehicle but it is in fact the 9T230 transloader vehicle, based on the same BAZ 6944 chassis. Close inspection will reveal that the after compartment is covered by a canvas tarpaulin and lacks several of the access panels of the launcher vehicle. This is a retired Czechoslovak vehicle. (Andrzej Kinski)

The only surviving Oka 9P71 launcher vehicles in the former USSR are at military museums. This 9P71 launcher vehicle is currently preserved at the Central Army Museum in Moscow. Unfortunately, the plexiglass windows have been covered over with sheet metal, which somewhat distorts the appearance of the vehicle.

A close-up of the suspension of the 9P71 TEL, with a view of the radiator grill above.

A detail view of the right side of the cab of the 9P71 launcher vehicle. (Andrzej Kinski)

A rear view of the 9P71 Oka missile launcher vehicle. The configuration is very similar to the 9P129. The Oka missile sits nearby. Notice that it uses the same griddle vanes as the 9M79 Tochka. This rear view also shows the covers for the waterjets under the rear hull.

A view of the radiator grill on the right side of the 9P71 Oka launcher vehicle.

With the demilitarization of the Oka due to the INF Treaty, Russia looked for a new Scud replacement. This emerged in 1999 as the Tender, also known by its export name of Iskander-E. The prototype was based on a BAZ truck much like the Oka's 9P71, but the production version is based on the much larger and heavier MZKT-79305 Astrolot truck. This enables the launch vehicle to carry and launch two complete missiles.

The SS-12 Scaleboard, called Temp by the Soviets, is a contemporary of the SS-1c Scud B and shares a very similar chassis. The Temp/Scaleboard has much greater range than the R-17/Scud. This is one of the initial production 2P11 launcher vehicles on parade in Moscow.

In the early 1980s, the Temp system was modernized by the development of a new missile, originally designated SS-22 by US intelligence. When it was realized that it was fired from essentially the same 2P19 launcher, it was redesignated as the SS-12b Scaleboard. In fact, the launcher is the improved 9P120, and the new system is designed as Temp-S. This system was retired due to the INF treaty, and a single 9P120 launcher and 9M76 missile are preserved in Moscow at the Central Army museum.

A left side view of the 9P120 Temp-S at the Moscow museum. There are some changes between the 9P120 launcher and the 9P117 (Scud) launcher. Notice, for example, the absence of the usual tool box between the first and second wheels found on the 9P117.

A side view of the 9M76 missile and the 9P120 Temp-S TEL vehicle.

On first glance, this appears to be a fuzzy photo of a 9P120 Temp-S launcher vehicle. In fact, it is the only unclassified photo of the Temp-S transloader vehicle. One of the few apparent differences between the transloader vehicle and the TEL is the lack of missile erection equipment at the very rear of the vehicle.

A rear view of the right side of the 9P120 Temp-S launcher vehicle. On this vehicle, the missile is entirely contained within an environmental canister until it is ready for launch. This permits temperature stabilization for the solid rocket motors.

A left rear view of the 9P120 Temp-S launcher vehicle. The 9M76 missile can be see in the foreground.

A closeup of the nose-cone of the 9M76 missile with the TEL in the background. The grill-work on the compartment behind the TEL's cab is essentially the same as on early production variants of the Scud TEL.

A close-up view of the area between the first and second stages of the 9M76 missile showing the unusual exhaust chambers and the characteristic griddle fins on the rear of the second stage.

A Russian missile crew loading the first and second stages of a 9M76 missile (minus the warhead) into its launcher canister.

`The RT-15 (SS-14 Scamp) was the first Soviet attempt to field a mobile strategic missile. The Obiekt 815 launcher vehicle is based on components of the IS heavy tank series. This is one of the early production TELs. This was an intermediate range missile system, intended for targets in Europe, Japan and China.

A rear view of the RT-15/SS-14 Scamp TEL. Although significantly larger than the Scud TEL, the Scamp TEL is very similar in overall conception.

The Obiekt 815 Scamp TEL underwent several variations during its development. This is the second and final TEL variant, which can be distinguished by its altered forward driver's station area.

The first successful Soviet mobile IRBM was the Pioner (Pioneer), better known in the West as the SS-20 Saber. The 15P72 TEL is based on the MAZ-547V heavy wheeled transporter. These systems were eliminated under the INF Treaty, and this survivor sits as a museum display at the Central Army Museum in Moscow.

A front view of the 15P72 Pioner TEL. The TEL cab bears obvious similarities to the earlier Scud and Scaleboard TELs. This launcher vehicle was developed by V. Sobolev's team of the Titan TsKB (Central Design Bureau) at the Barrikady Plant in Volgograd which developed many of the Soviet missile TEL launcher systems. The Barrikady Plant is probably better known to military historians for its role in producing T-34 tanks during the crucial battle of Stalingrad (now called Volgograd) in World War 2.

A rear view of the 15P72 Pioner TEL. The development of this IRBM led to considerable political controversy in Europe, eventually resulting in the deployment of US Army Pershing missiles in the mid-1980s.

An official Soviet photo showing the 15P72 Pioner TEL without the launch canister. The missile is shipped in the launch canister, so when not armed, the TEL lacks the canister. Note the right cab area in comparison to the cab on the transloader.

A rare view of an RSD-10 Pioner missile being prepared for firing. This photo shows the undercarriage of the launch cradle. Notice that the circular dome cover for the missile launch tube has been left in front of the vehicle. The missile's triple warhead can be seen at the end of the tube.

The Pioner transloader is very similar to the TEL vehicle. One of the distinguishing features is the right cab, which is a mirror image of the left cab. On the TEL the cab is considerably different in shape.

Each Pioner launcher battalion is equipped with a command & control vehicle, based on a modified MAZ-7910 chassis. This vehicle contains the command staff for operating the missiles when they are deployed in the field.

A 15Zh45 Pioner missile seconds after launch. The canister ejects the missile using gas pressure, at which time the missile engine ignites.

The 15Zh45 Pioner missile. A single missile was provided to the United States for a display celebrating the INF Treaty. Currently preserved at the National Air & Space Museum in Washington, DC, the RSD-10 is placed alongside a Pershing II missile, the type eliminated by the US side for the INF Treaty. The 15Zh45 uses a solid-propellant rocket engine, and the solid propellant segments are all carefully labeled in alphabetical order in the Cyrillic alphabet from A to I on the second stage and A to L on the first stage.

A close-up of the 15P72 Pioner TEL. When in service, the TEL usually has additional stowage immediately forward the right cab.

A close-up view of the front three wheels of the 15P72 Pioner TEL showing the forward stabilization pad in the down position.

A detail view of the rear three road wheels as well as the launcher control panel compartments above.

A close-up on the very unusual post-boost bus (PBV) with its multiple independently targeted warheads (MIRV). Each of these conical warheads would contain a large thermonuclear warhead on an operational missile capable of destroying a small city. Most American missiles have a ballistic cover over this section, but not some Russian types.

A close-up of the first stage and base of the 15Zh45 missile. The characteristic Belotserkovskiy grid fins are evident in this view. On launch, these would pop out to help stabilize the missile.

The crew of an 15P72 Pioner open the special launcher hanger doors for a 15P72 Pioner TEL to emerge. (Sovfoto)

A rare inside view of the launcher-hanger of the Pioner. The Topol uses a similar type of Krona structure. (Sovfoto)

The massive 15P72 TEL vehicle of the Pioner (SS-20 Saber) IRBM system. The building behind it is the special Krona launch shelter for housing these mobile launchers. In the event of an emergency, the roofs of these buildings open and the missiles can be fired from within the building. (Sovfoto)

The RT-20P (SS-15 Scrooge) was the first Soviet attempt at a mobile intercontinental ballistic missile in the early 1960s. It was not successful, and the program was cancelled in October 1969. The launcher vehicle, designated the Obiekt 821, is based on components from the T-10 heavy tank series.

A side view of the RT-20P's Obiekt 821 TEL. Although based on IS heavy tank components, the TEL is considerably larger than tactical TELs of the period such as the 2P19 Scud TEL.

A rear view of the RT-20P's Obiekt 821 TEL showing the enormous stabilizing arms used to lock down the chassis during launch.

The first successful Soviet mobile ICBM is the Topol (Poplar Tree), known in the West as the SS-25 Sickle. The MAZ-7917 TEL bears a close resemblance to the 15P72 Pioner TEL, which is not surprising as both are based on MAZ heavy trucks and the launchers were both developed by the Titan TsKB at the Barrikady Plant in Volgograd. The Topol is basically a modernized and enlarged Pioner with a third stage added.

Several Topol on display in Moscow in 1990. The Topol is deployed at several former Pioner bases, using the same type of environmental shelter/hanger. This particular TEL is the type called "Raznovidnost A", Version A by the Russians.

As in the case of the Pioner, the Topol TEL has stabilizing pads at the very rear of the vehicle, and midways down the side behind the second axle.

The latest Russian missile system is the Topol-M, known in the West as SS-27. It is a further evolution of the Topol, but larger. A mobile version has been planned, and the prototype was built on the MAZ-79221 truck chassis as seen here. This superficially resembles the earlier Topol TEL on the MAZ-7917, but it has eight axles rather than seven.

The FKR-2 (SSC-1a Sepal) was originally deployed in the Soviet Air Force as a theatre nuclear delivery weapon. Although it's 2P30 TEL bears little resemblance to the FROG-7's 9P113 TEL, in fact they are both based on the same ZIL-135 chassis. The 2P30 uses the ZIL-135MB chassis.

A rear view of the 2P30 TEL. The circular protrusions on the top of the missile tubes accommodate the hemispherical launch container end plates when the tube is opened. These missiles were not deployed in large numbers.

SPU-35V Redut (SSC-1B Shaddock)

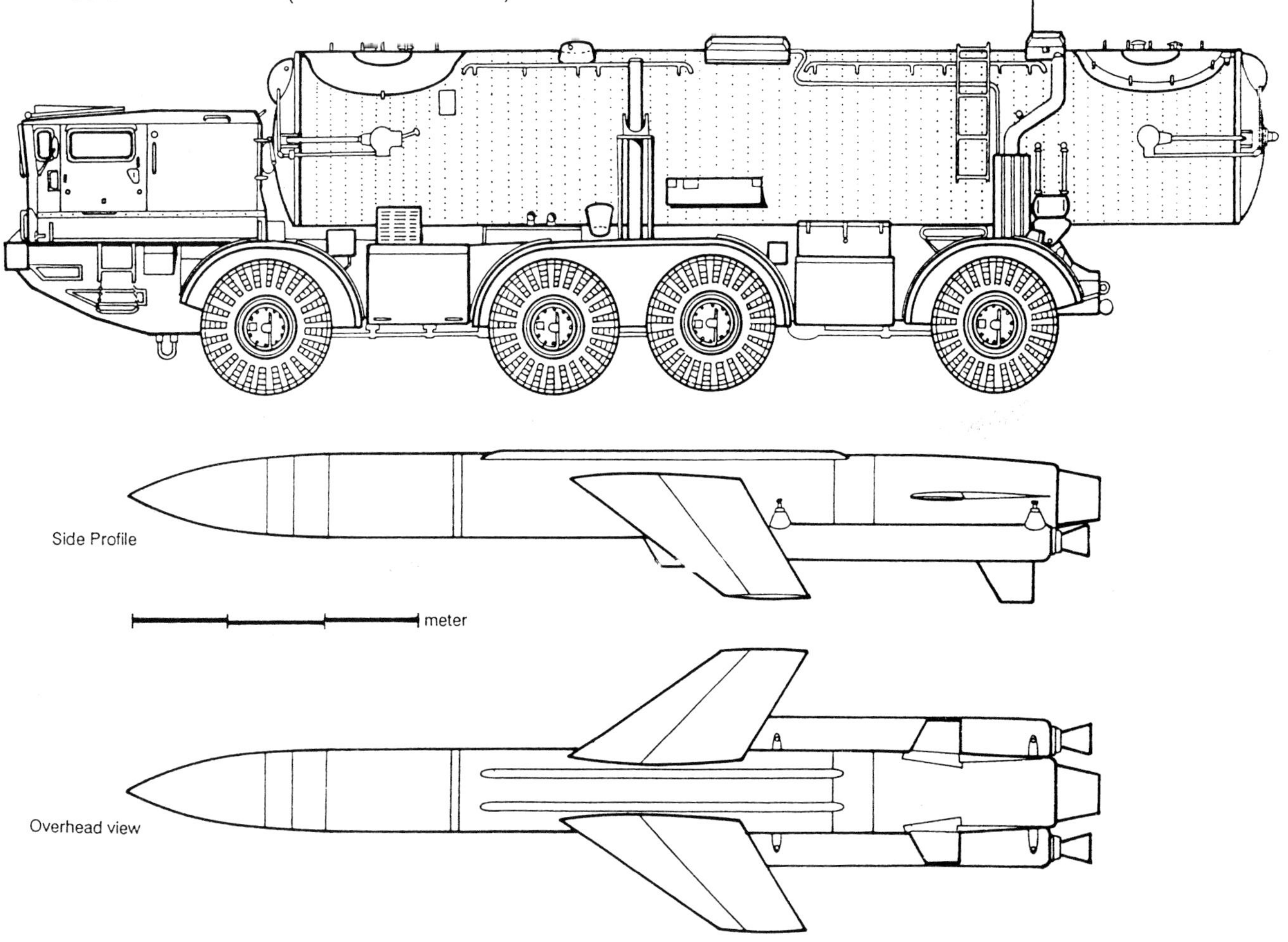

Side Profile

meter

Overhead view

The Soviet Navy acquired an anti-ship version of the FKR-2 system called the Redut (SSC-1b Shaddock). It was similar to the Air Force FKR-2 system, but the cab designs were significantly different. The coastal defense version of the launcher was called the SPU-35V. These served with the Soviet Navy's BRAV coastal defense units starting in the 1960s.

Long one of the most secret Soviet vehicles, the SPU-243 is the launcher for the Tupolev VR-3 Reys (Journey) reconnaissance drone system. This is based on the same TEL chassis as the 2P30 Progress and Redut, but launches a Tupolev Tu-143 reconnaissance drone rather than a cruise missile.

An interesting rear view of a SPU-35V Redut TEL being erected by a Navy crew for launch. The canister is near maximum elevation in this view. The associated S-35 missile is a common naval anti-ship cruise missile used on many Soviet cruisers.

This rear view of the SPU-243 shows the characteristic container lids, and the Tu-143 drone can be seen poking out the back of the launcher. The VR-3 systems are deployed under air force control and a drone reconnaissance squadron has four SPU-243 launcher vehicles capable of launching about 20 missions per day.

A SPU-243 Reys launcher in launch position. The system is still widely used by the Russian Air Force and by other air forces of the former Soviet Union. It was exported to several of the former Warsaw Pact countries in the early 1980s including Czechoslovakia and Romania. The Reys was supplied to Syria in 1984 and has been used over Israel. Iraq also obtained the system for reconnaissance flights over Iran during the Iran-Iraq war in the 1980s.

A view inside the launch tube shows the Tu-143 drone. A new version of the drone, the Tu-300, can be used as a UCAV (uninhabited combat air vehicle) to deliver cluster bombs against targets and then return back to base.

The Redut was succeeded in 1978 by the 4K51 Rubezh system, known in NATO as SSC-3 Styx. The 3P51 launcher vehicle is based on the MAZ-543M, similar to the vehicle used with the Scud TEL, but without a crew cab on the right side. The command center is located immediately behind the cab, and the KT-161 missile launchers behind that section. This is a 3P51M Rubezh-A TEL of the German Kusten-Verteidigungsraketen-Regiment "Waldemar Verner" KRR 18, stationed at Schwarzenpfost near Rostock. (Jürgen Plate via Michael Jerchel)

A 3P51M Rubezh-A launcher vehicle of the KRR 18 in transit mode with its Garpun-E (Plank Shave) radar folded and launch canisters in travel position. The insignia of KRR 18 was a yellow anchor painted on the vehicle side. These missiles have been retired from service in Germany but are still in use by Russia, Ukraine and other foreign customers. (Jürgen Plate via Michael Jerchel)

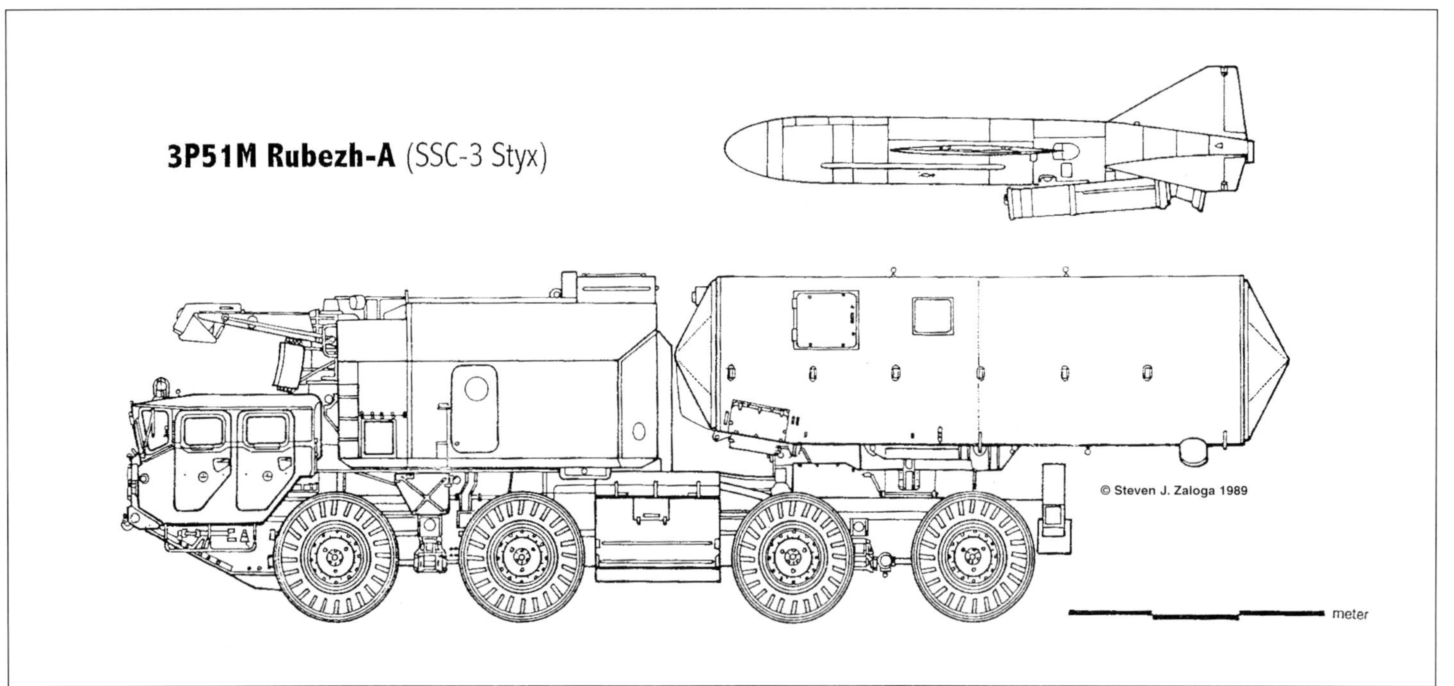

A 3P51M Rubezh-A launcher of the KRR 18 in transit mode with the Garpun-E radar folded. The missile used by this system is the P-20 and P-21, known more commonly as the Styx. (Jürgen Plate via Michael Jerchel)

A rear view of the 3P51M Rubezh-A launcher vehicle of KRR 18 before the retirement of the system. Each launcher has two KT-161 launch containers. (Jürgen Plate via Michael Jerchel)

A detail shot of the chassis and lower portions of the launcher for the 3P51M Rubezh-A launcher.

The 3P51M Rubezh-A coastal anti-ship missile launcher is based on the MAZ-7910 truck, very similar to the 9P117 used with the Scud B except for the absence of an auxiliary cab on the right side.

One of the rarest of the Soviet cruise missiles launchers was the S-10 Granat system (SSC-4 Slingshot) which fired an intermediate range cruise missile much like the American Tomahawk GLCM. A view of the 3M12 cruise missile is inset. This particular system was only beginning to enter service in the late 1980s when the INF Treaty came into effect, and all the systems were demilitarized as a result before fully entering service.